EARL ANTHONY'S
CHAMPIONSHIP
BOWLING

EARL ANTHONY'S
CHAMPIONSHIP
BOWLING

EARL ANTHONY
WITH DAWSON TAYLOR

Contemporary Books, Inc.
Chicago

Library of Congress Cataloging in Publication Data

Anthony, Earl, 1938–
   Earl Anthony's championship bowling.

   Bibliography: p.
   Includes index.
   1. Bowling.   I. Taylor, Dawson.   II. Title.
III. Title: Championship bowling.
GV903.A55   1983   794.6   83-15434
ISBN 0-8092-5490-5

Published by Contemporary Books, Inc.
180 North Michigan Avenue, Chicago, Illinois 60601
Manufactured in the United States of America
Library of Congress Catalog Card Number: 83-15434
International Standard Book Number: 0-8092-5490-5

Published simultaneously in Canada by Beaverbooks, Ltd.
195 Allstate Parkway, Valleywood Business Park
Markham, Ontario L3R 4T8 Canada

CONTENTS

ACKNOWLEDGMENTS

We would like to express our thanks and sincere appreciation to our bowling friends who helped immeasurably to bring this book to completion: our bowling models—Catherine Schlegel, Jason and Brendalee Croce, Scott Haefele, and William Walker; and our great photographers—Ray Glonka, Roy De Fillipis, Joaquin Bengochea, and Barbara Spigner. We are grateful to Steve Croce for allowing us to use his Garden Lanes in North Palm Beach, Florida, for our photographic sequences. We also thank Bill Taylor and Larry Lichstein for sharing their expert knowledge of how a bowling ball performs.

Earl Anthony
Dawson Taylor

NOTE FOR THE READER

You have, no doubt, seen me perform in the past years on the Professional Bowlers Tour which is televised nationally on Saturday afternoons. I am sure you will recall that I am a left-handed bowler; yet in this book you will see me pictured as a right-hander. This is done intentionally. There are approximately 95 right-handed bowlers to every 5 left-handed bowlers in this country; so, since 95 percent of my potential readers are right-handed, the editors and I thought it best in many cases for the photographer to "flop the negatives" of the pictures; that is, reverse them in order to show how I would look if I were bowling right-handed.

Incidentally, all the photos are action photos—they were taken while I was actually bowling. There are no posed shots other than the obvious ones showing me in the act of teaching or pointing out some important point about the bowling lane itself.

There are many technical terms in bowling; many words common to other sports; and many ordinary words such as strike, spare, and frame that have a special meaning when applied to bowling. I have included a chapter on the language of bowling showing how it is used during actual play. I have also added a comprehensive glossary at the end of the book which will help you understand terms you will encounter in the wonderful sport of bowling. I recommend that you turn to the glossary first to familiarize yourself with the bowling vocabulary. Then you will be better prepared to read this book—which I hope will prove to be the best ever written on the art, science, and psychology of bowling.

Earl Anthony

To Susie, my wife, my best friend.

Earl Anthony

To the memory of George M. Taylor,
Hanley Taylor, and Marr Taylor,
the great bowlers of the Taylor Family.

Dawson Taylor

1
THE SECRET
OF EXPLOSIVE
BOWLING ACTION

This chapter presents the important technique known as "the squeeze," which is the secret to achieving the explosive strike ball—one that "blows the pins into the pit."

There is one and only one secret of the explosive action of the bowling ball as it hits the 1–3 pocket and causes a strike. It is called the squeeze. *The bowler must use* squeeze *finger action* as he releases the ball.

Squeeze finger action is very close to the finger action that occurs when you snap your fingers strongly. To understand the concept put your thumb against your joined third and fourth fingers and snap them as hard as you can. Notice how the fingers close against your palm and how your thumb moves forward.

Here are three successive views of my application of squeeze finger action as I deliver the ball over the foul line. In this, the first, notice that my hand is still in the ball as I approach the delivery point. My thumb is pointing inward toward the pins and my fingers are behind the ball. My fingers are ready to squeeze the moment my thumb has come out of the ball.

Here is the second view of the delivery. My thumb has already come out of the ball and the ball remains on my fingers. The fingers are preparing to squeeze as they deliver the ball straight forward down my target line.

Here is the third view of the delivery with my fingers closing in the squeeze action, my thumb forward on the inside, and the ball clearly on its way down the line with squeeze action imparted to it. You can clearly see that the thumb hole of the ball has rotated from behind the ball to the opposite side at about a 10 o'clock spot on a clock dial.

Here is another view, visualized without the ball. This picture shows the position of the hand just as the ball is about to be released with squeeze finger action. The thumb is on the inside; the fingers are firm but have not yet imparted the squeeze.

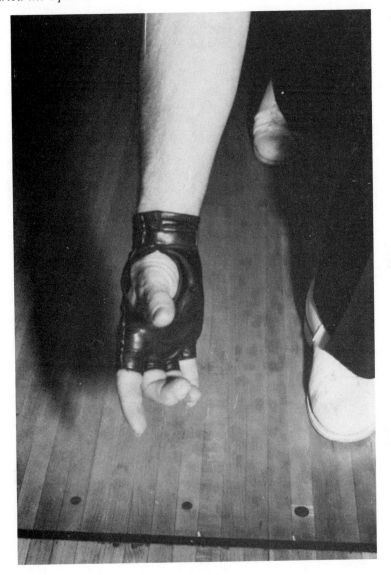

Here is a subsequent view, again visualized without the ball. The fingers are closing against the palm and the thumb is coming forward to meet them as the squeeze action is completed. It is the squeezing fingers that put the action on the ball—the stronger the closing of the fingers, the stronger the action on the ball.

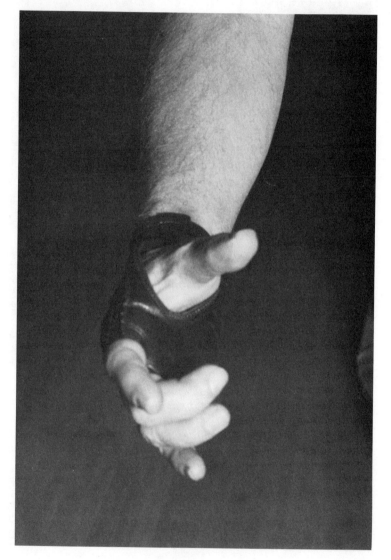

2
EXERCISES TO PERFECT THE SECRET

Here are a few simple exercises for you to perform both with and without your bowling ball in order to help you understand the secret of the squeeze action in the bowling delivery.

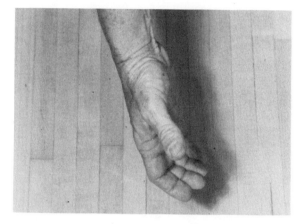

Put your bowling hand in front of you in an imaginary grip of the ball. Let your third and fourth fingers be firm and your thumb relaxed.

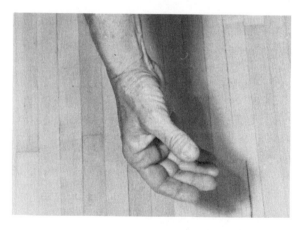

Close your hand slowly and observe that as your fingers move toward your palm your thumb wants to move forward out of their way. In the actual bowling delivery the ball would be on the fingers. Try to see it in your imagination coming off the fingers.

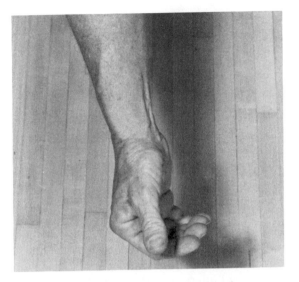

Now the fingers are closed even farther toward the ultimate squeeze. See the thumb moving forward but still on a line toward the left. Perform this hand movement over and over in order to impress upon your mind the finger action that must take place inside the bowling ball for an explosive delivery.

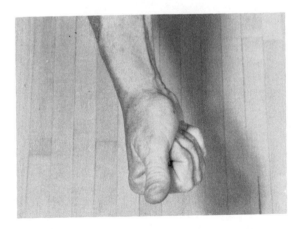

Here is the final view of the clenched hand, the squeeze completed. The thumb has come forward; the fingers are tight against the palm. The tension in the inner forearm can be clearly seen, too, as evidence of the strength of the squeeze the fingers have imparted to the ball.

Here are some exercises that will help you to understand squeeze finger action and perfect it in your own delivery. Begin by putting your bowling ball on the floor in front of you and insert your third and fourth fingers in their finger holds. Leave your thumb outside the ball.

Second, turn the ball into the position shown in this photograph. Leave your thumb outside the ball but on the side of it. Let your fingers be in their finger holes and tensed, ready to close in the squeeze finger action. With your thumb still outside of the ball, perform the squeeze with your fingers and let the ball run to the left, as it will once the action is imparted to it. The distance it runs is an indication of the strength and power of your squeeze.

The final part of this exercise is to begin performing it with your thumb inserted part way into the thumb hole and then, finally, with your thumb all the way into the thumb hole. By doing this exercise frequently you will perfect the marvelous "finger sense" of the ball release. Begin by lifting your thumb and inserting it part way into the ball.

Here are two views of the squeeze finger action being imparted to a bowling ball that will be delivered over the line and will be rotating on a 4 o'clock–10 o'clock axis. Note the white arrow in the first picture. The fingers and thumb are still in the ball but about to release it with the squeeze.

Here is the second view of the ball starting its revolution on a 4 o'clock–10 o'clock axis. Notice that the thumb is well out of the ball and coming forward while the fingers are still in the ball to the last split second. The white arrow is starting to disappear around the other side of the ball showing that the squeeze action has begun.

Here are two successive views of a delivery that would cause the ball to rotate on a 5 o'clock–11 o'clock axis after it has left the fingers. In the first the thumb is still inside the ball but pointing to 11 o'clock. The fingers, also inside the ball, are in a 5 o'clock position behind the ball.

Here is that same 5 o'clock–11 o'clock delivery a fraction of a second after the thumb has come out of the ball. The fingers are still in it and beginning their squeeze action. You can see the white arrow heading for 11 o'clock. Although the ball rotates on an axis to the left, the hand and arm come straight up and follow through straight down the target line.

3
THE SEVEN
FUNDAMENTALS OF
CHAMPIONSHIP BOWLING

There are seven basic fundamentals to an effective, repeatedly explosive bowling delivery that results in strikes, and also gives the bowler the ability to convert spares and many splits with regularity so as to achieve a high bowling average.

These basic fundamentals are:

1. Relaxation
2. Rhythm and Timing
3. Squareness to the Line and Ability to Hit the Target
4. Correct Ball Fit and Ball Balance
5. Application of Squeeze Action
6. Consistent Wrist Action and Full Follow-Through
7. Speed Control

In the following pages I have used my own style of bowling as a model for you to study and, if you care to, imitate. In Chapter 21 I point out that everyone must develop his or her own bowling style, so I do not recommend slavish imitation of my own delivery. There is no question, however, that in order to become a good to great bowler you must obey every one of the seven fundamentals of championship bowling.

Before we discuss the seven fundamentals in detail let's take a look at my own bowling style. As you know, it has been quite successful for me.

RELAXATION

We have already discussed the finger and wrist action which puts explosive dynamic power into the 1–3 pocket and results in a strike. Now let's examine the jigsaw puzzle of the delivery.

Every element of the seven basic fundamentals of championship bowling must be present in order for the bowling delivery to work. The first fundamental is *relaxation*. You must learn to relax your body, your bowling arm, your hand, and your wrist in order to bowl your best. I will grant you that in tournament competition or even close league competitions this may be difficult for the ordinary bowler to accomplish.

As I start my delivery I hold the ball outstretched in front of me at about shoulder height. I concentrate on my target out on the lanes. Everything I do is aimed at hitting that target as accurately as I can. By holding my ball out in front of me this way I am able to let it drop away into its backswing without any unnecessary moves of the ball either toward me or away from me. It simply drops away of its own momentum into what is called a pendulum *swing, a downward arc that lasts until the ball reaches the top of my backswing and then makes a similar forward arc toward the delivery point as the ball passes my sliding foot at the foul line.*

The first step is taken with my right foot. I have the sensation of pushing the ball simultaneously away from my body. My foot and the ball go into motion at precisely the same moment. The weight of the ball is still being helped by my left hand but the right hand is getting ready to take over.

On my second step, taken with my left foot, I am allowing the ball to drop naturally into its backswing. The ball will be passing my body just as my left foot touches the approach. Notice that my left hand has left the ball now and that my left arm has begun to swing out from my side to begin its task of helping my body balance.

Now the ball is at midpoint in the downswing. My left hand and arm have moved farther out in their balancing act. Notice that I have begun to lean forward in my delivery and that I am concentrating intensely on my target out on the lane.

On my third step the ball reaches the top of my backswing. Notice that my arm is absolutely straight and is swinging from my shoulder in a pendulumlike motion. Once again I call your attention to my concentration on my target out on the lane.

Now the ball is midway in its downswing and I am approaching the "moment of truth," the explosion point of the delivery of the ball out over the foul line straight at my target down on the lane. Notice that I have leaned even farther forward and that my left leg is bent as the left foot slides straight toward the line. Also note that my fingers are on the side of the ball and behind my thumb. I am almost ready to give the ball the squeeze action.

Here is the squeeze finger action as seen just before the explosion point of the delivery. My fingers are behind my thumb. If you look closely you can see that my thumb is partway out of the thumb hole and the fingers are now carrying the whole weight of the ball for the final few seconds of the delivery. Observe the squareness of my shoulders to the line and again, my intense concentration on my target.

Here is a view taken from down the lane showing the squeeze action a fraction of a second after it has been applied to the ball at the explosion point of the delivery. Notice that the ball has begun to turn, as the finger holes are clearly evident on the left-hand side of the ball. Notice the closed fingers and the full follow-through as my arm and hand come straight up my target line. Notice, too, that I am staying down at the line.

Here is an excellent view of my delivery from the side. The ball has not yet touched down on the lane. I believe in getting the ball well out on the lane under most circumstances in order to ensure that I have followed through and in order to make sure that I have imparted the necessary finger squeeze action after my thumb has left the ball.

Now that the ball has been delivered, the right hand and arm continue straight up in a decided lifting motion. This move, coupled with the squeeze finger action at the line, ensures that the ball will have the explosive action needed at the pins. It is of paramount importance that the bowler stay down at the line as long as he can. Notice how far forward I have bent and that my eyes are still intent upon my target.

As I take my stance for delivery I am visualizing my target line down the lane. As you can see from this photo there is an optical illusion called the effect of parallax. *My eyes are to the left of the target line, but my shoulder, arm, and hand are in line with it. I must have the courage of my convictions and put the ball down the true target line and let the action on the ball do the work at the pocket.*

Here is an excellent view of my delivery long after the ball has left my hand and is traveling down the lane. If you look closely you can see that it has made one full revolution already, as the finger holes are coming up for the second time on the right side of the ball. Notice how I have held my delivery at the line, how my hand and arm have come straight up toward my target, and how I am still leaning far forward, staying with the ball.

Relaxation begins with the way you take your grip on the bowling ball. With a relaxed wrist, slap your ball a couple of times before you insert your fingers into their holes. Put your thumb in last and rehearse its quick exit by making sure it is free and ready to get out ahead of the fingers so they can squeeze on their way out. Look closely at my forefinger in this photo. You can see no evidence of tension at all.

I have some simple suggestions for you to help you relax when you are bowling. If you follow these faithfully you will be more relaxed and, knowing that you are, you will bowl better.

Here's how to relax your grip: Just before you insert your fingers into the finger holes, slap the ball gently. Pat it several times as if it were a baby. Always place your fingers in the holes first and then insert your thumb. This practice will help to keep you concentrating on the need for finger action at release (explained earlier). It will also rid you of the fear that your thumb is buried in its thumb hole. Watch the good bowlers and oftentimes you can see them practicing the thumb release as they prepare to make a bowling delivery.

Your wrist must be firm, not loose; relaxed and yet not tense. You should feel the firmness in the outside of your arm and along the straight line from the back of your hand past your wrist and up your forearm. Your arm is definitely looser than your wrist. Basil "Buzz" Fazio, a great bowler on the Stroh team, used to claim that his arm was as "limp as a dishrag" when he was bowling his best.

Now, about relaxing your body: Break your knees slightly when you assume your starting position. Take a tip from the great golfers and "sit down" a little to ease tension in your body. Before you make up your mind to start your pushaway, look to your right and to your left to make sure that no other bowler is going to disturb your concentration. Don't make one step into your starting position until you are completely convinced (and therefore relaxed about it) that no other bowler is going to upset your concentration by picking up his ball from the rack, by body gyrations at a nearby line, or by any other distraction. Thus you will be assured of a relaxed delivery free of disturbances.

Now that you are ready to bowl, take a deep breath, hold it for a second longer than normal, and then exhale slowly. At the moment you complete your exhalation, go! Physiologists have proven that your body cannot be tense immediately after the exhalation of a deep breath. This tip alone will save you a great deal of anguish in competitive bowling. Your arm is relaxed, your body is relaxed, and the result is a smooth relaxed delivery of the ball out over the foul line. Continue the feeling of relaxation by letting your right hand, right arm, and right shoulder follow through freely out over the line. You will find, as I have, that the ball seems to sense a relaxed delivery and picks up more energy than usual. In bowling, the expression used about a relaxed bowler is that "he is free-wheeling it." That is the feeling I want you to have when you are bowling.

Remember the first fundamental: *relaxation*. It applies to every shot you make, no matter how difficult. Relax and you will score better, I promise you.

RHYTHM AND TIMING

The second fundamental of championship bowling is *rhythm and timing*. Let's go to the dictionary for the precise meaning of *timing* as it applies to bowling. Webster says: "It is the art or practice of regulating the speed of a motion or stroke so as to cause it to achieve its maximum effectiveness at the correct moment."

In bowling, of course, this means that the bowler must put the ball in motion at the start of his four- or five-step delivery toward the foul line, and at the same time that his feet are moving toward the line arrange to have his bowling arm take the ball backward to a stop in his backswing and then downward in a forward swing that will allow his arm and the ball to catch up to his last step as he slides with a bent knee toward the foul line. The word for this timing in bowling is *synchronization*. The double movement of the body in forward step motion must be absolutely synchronized to coincide with that last step as the bowler slides toward the line. The arm swing cannot be too slow or too fast or the two events—the bowler's sliding foot nearing the line and the bottom of the arc of the ball in the bowler's hand—will not *mesh*, or synchronize. Without exact timing there is no possibility of the bowler delivering a consistently effective ball. Certainly, he will roll a ball down the lane in some fashion but the result will never be satisfactory.

Here are a few ideas to help you achieve good timing in your delivery. My first and best advice to all bowlers is "Take your time." Don't rush the line. Take your first step slowly and gradually increase your speed until you come to the foul line. An ancient bowling adage that remains good advice today is "Concentrate on taking your second step slowly and then you will *have* to make your first step slow!"

Your ability to time your delivery so that your hand and arm reach the foul line precisely as your sliding foot reaches it, too, depends a great part on timing your pushaway.

You may start the ball waist-high or chest-high or throw it way up in the air as Don Carter used to do. You may hold the ball at belt-height and push it straight out. You may suspend it in front of you and let it drop away directly into its arc. You may even stand and let it dangle at arm's end, pumping it back and forth until you sense that you are ready to go.

All of these suggestions lead to this advice. You must find the best way that you and you alone can time your pushaway so that when you reach the foul line, sliding smoothly with your left foot, the hand and arm are just passing your left foot. If you have a four-step delivery—and most classic bowlers do—make your push coincide exactly with your first step.

If you find that you are getting to the line too soon with the ball, lengthen your pushaway by starting it higher. If you are there too late, shorten it by starting it lower. Remember, too, that your pushaway can be speeded up by an actual *push* down as you start the ball away from your body into its backswing. In general, the same rules prevail for speeding up or slowing down the bowling arc for bowlers who take five steps or more. No matter how many steps you take you must time your last several steps and your slide so that your arm and ball are just passing your left heel at the moment of ball delivery at the foul line.

In working on your timing I suggest that you work out your own individual count, your *mantra.* Say it to yourself mentally when you make a bowling delivery. Let it be "one, two, three, slide" or "five, four, three, two, go" or something similar. There are electric devices called *metronomes* for musicians. Such a timer can be set to whatever rhythm you want and can work wonders in developing a consistently timed bowling delivery.

Remember the first two fundamentals now: *relaxation* and *rhythm and timing*.

SQUARENESS TO THE LINE AND ABILITY TO HIT THE TARGET

Squareness to the Line

Eddie Lubanski, a great bowler of the Stroh beer team in the '60s, was a well known horseshoe pitching champion. Early in my own career I was fortunate enough to see Lubanski in action in an American Bowling Congress tournament. I was struck by the remarkably strong, straight follow-through Eddie used, and when I pointed it out to a friend of mine I was told about his other successful career in the game of horseshoes. I added a worthy bit of knowledge to my bowling technique. I would try to imitate Lubanski's style of delivery and his follow-through and see what happened.

The result was that I proved to myself how important it is that the body be *square to the line* as the arm went through its pitching motion. I had pitched horseshoes myself when I was young. I still had the mental picture of the body square to the line of flight, the free and easy backswing and follow-through, and the lift of the hand as it released the shoe on its way to the stake in the pit.

More and more as I continued to practice my bowling I had a mental picture of the great horseshoe pitcher. I kept my hips and shoulders square to my line, and I followed through with my hand and arms straight down my target line. I pretended to myself that I was not rolling a bowling ball, but pitching a horseshoe.

The results were most satisfactory. My ball had action at the pins. It seemed to lose action when I tried to force it into the pocket instead of letting it go straightaway. My conclusion was and still is in this advice I give to you about the fundamentals of championship bowling: Your body, your shoulders, and your hips all must have a sense of squareness to the line in order for the bowling delivery to attain its maximum effectiveness, its greatest power.

When you line yourself up for your normal strike shot I want you to go through this mental routine: With your left foot on the center dot, your right shoulder, arm, and bowling swing will be in a direct line with a board which runs between the second and third arrows at the break of the boards.

I want you to visualize a white line or a black line (whichever color your imagination prefers) running straight back from the space through the foul line to your hand, your arm, and the arc of your bowling swing. As you stand readying yourself to make a delivery I want you to feel the right angles your entire body, your shoulders, and your hips make with that imaginary line running toward you. And as you proceed into a bowling delivery I want you to feel that all the while your ball is in its backswing and downswing, your body is still attempting as well as it can to maintain that squareness to the line.

I promise you that if you will visualize that imaginary line and obey my instructions to feel your squareness to it during your delivery, you will have as powerful a strike ball as you can possibly get.

Ability to Hit the Target

You may have the greatest ability in the bowling world to roll an explosive bowling ball, but if you do not understand where you should direct it you will never achieve high scores. First, the good bowler must be able to determine what his target is and second, he must be able to hit that target consistently.

I would like to explain what I call the *target line* in bowling. Going back into bowling history, you may recall in the early days of bowling there were no markers or arrows on the lanes to help a bowler sight his target.

There always was a *splice,* or *break of the boards* out on the lanes where the maple and pine boards dovetail. Usually some of those boards would be darker than others and so the bowlers of that day would roll for, say, the "second board to the right of that dark board." Sometimes, too, the "piano keys" were all of the same color and then the bowler really had trouble finding his target line.

Then in the post World War II period came the innovation of the arrows, darts, and dots placed in the bed of the lane approach and out on the lane itself. At least the bowler had a recognizable target and target line that he could use to organize his approach to the strike line, and also a great benefit—an added ability to organize his spare shooting.

Let me take you now out onto the lanes and explain how you will be able to use these wonderful markers to find your target and target line (see picture).

Here is a photo of the arrows out on the lane to help you determine your target line. Each arrow, or dart as it is sometimes called, is five boards apart. Bowlers count from the channel in to designate a particular board. The wide black arrow I have applied to the lane indicates the usual track for most bowlers who roll a normal hook. It is centered on the 12 board. You will learn to roll your ball over a particular board. You should learn to call it by name.

First, you will note that there are round black dots embedded in the approach area, usually one at the three-step line and one at the four-step line. These are meant to give you a method of locating what I call your target foot (if you are right-handed, your left). Face the pins squarely and place your left foot directly behind the center dot. You will notice

On nearly every lane, if you will examine the surface carefully near the arrows and in the area leading to the arrows you will notice that part of the lane is darker or dirtier than the rest of the lane. That indicates the worn track that most of the balls pass over. Go out onto the lane and look for it. The knowledge of where it is may help you to decide your target line.

Here is another demonstration of squaring toward the target. This is an inside shot, that is, the ball will be put down to the left of the center of the lane but will travel out toward a spot between the second and third arrows. Once more, note the squareness of my body to that intended line, the follow-through straight down that line, and the concentration on the target spot at the break of the boards.

that your right arm and the right side of your body are lined up with a board which runs between the second and third arrows from the right-hand side of the lane.

Before you roll your first ball of the day, you should look down the lane and choose one particular board that runs between the second and third arrows and then, in your mind's eye, draw a straight line back through the foul line. That imaginary line becomes your temporary target line. Your left foot should be used as your pointer. I call it my target foot because it aims at my target down the lane. You should always place it on the same dot in the approach. This beginning dot will be at the center of the lane or somewhere near the center; what dot you use will depend upon your ability to put action on the ball. The bowler with a strong hook might consistently start from the boards to the left of center; the bowler with a weaker ball might start two or more boards to the right of center.

Remember that I am discussing basic bowling fundamentals in this situation. My chapter on bowling in your own style will tell you about revising and adjusting to advice which tells you arbitrarily to "put your target foot on this spot, bowl down this line."

Always start from the same position and roll over the same board at the break of the boards down the same line until you have had an opportunity to observe whether your normal ball is hitting the pocket. Then, if any adjustment is necessary, a good rule to follow is, "Always move with your error."

That means that if your ball is crossing too high on the headpin, or to the left, you will move your starting position to the left (your error is to the left, remember). If you move to the left at the start and roll over the same target at the splice, your ball will tend to go farther to the right and should come into the pocket.

A good rule to follow is, "Never move your position more than a half a board or a board at a time." Always keep an accurate track in your mind of the starting position you last used or else you will become hopelessly confused. The bowler's expression for such confusion is, "He's really lost out there, he's fishing." Which means that the bowler is moving all over the lane in an unorganized fashion in a panic trying to find a suitable target line for himself.

The reverse strategy applies when your ball is not coming up to the headpin or is missing on the right. When that happens, move your beginning position slightly to the right, keeping your normal spot between the arrows as the pivot point between the approach and the pins.

There are other adjustments, too, that you will use in correcting your target line: the speed of the ball, the distance beyond the foul line where you first put your ball down, where it begins to roll on its axis, and most important, the amount of action your fingers impart to the ball at release.

Every bowler should work hard in finding his normal strike line and target at the break of the boards. By *normal* strike line I mean the starting position and spot at the splice down which the bowler delivers his normal active ball with customary speed, a ball that frequently results in a strike for him.

Squareness to the line and ability to hit the target is the third fundamental of championship bowling.

CORRECT BALL FIT AND BALL BALANCE

According to the outstanding expert in bowling ball drilling, Bill Taylor of Anaheim, California, there are 12 different individual measurements which must be taken into consideration in order to drill a bowling ball that fits the bowler.

And yet this statement of fact does not take into consideration *ball balance*. The weighing of a bowling ball in ounce or half-ounce increments on the top, the bottom, and one side or the other so as to create an allowable inbalance of dynamic weight is known as *ball balance*. There are literally thousands of different ball balances which can be added to the 12 basic individual finger and hand measurements.

If you told 20 different bowlers to hold out their hands for inspection you would see an amazing variety in human anatomy. Fingers are thin, fingers are fat, fingers are short, fingers are long. In some hands the thumb lies at a 50-degree angle with the forefinger. Another bowler's thumb lies back at a startling 5 or 10 degrees beyond the 90-degree mark.

This discussion of various hands is preliminary to my statement that in order to get a bowling ball that fits *your* hand—your individual hand with the short fingers but the long thumb—you must consult your "Doctor of Bowling," the professional ball driller. In every part of the

Tom Shockley, one of the best ball drillers in the business, is showing the equipment to measure dynamic balance of a bowling ball. The ball in the photo is in zero balance according to the scale, but if it were turned to either side it would be out of balance by one-half ounce, as indicated by the white marks on the ball. The white mark on the bottom of the photo shows side weight.

country there is such a man. I have never heard of a woman ball driller but perhaps there is one and I am not aware of her. The professional ball driller usually has had years of experience. In many cases he is a good bowler himself, often carrying a 200 average or more, so he knows the problems and solutions to fitting a proper bowling ball to your hand.

I will tell you a few of the things you will experience in ball fit as you learn to bowl better and better. Most bowlers begin their careers with a *house ball,* one of the free or rental balls supplied by the lane owner to accommodate the bowler who does not own his own ball. House balls are drilled in what is called *conventional three finger* style. That means that the bowler's fingers go into the holes up to the first knuckle, with the thumb all the way in.

Often the thumb hole on such a ball is much too large for the bowler, and the result is that he keeps dropping the ball at the foul line or even earlier in his delivery. After the bowler decides to take up bowling seriously he should get his own ball, one drilled to fit him and no one else.

A good ball driller will take your finger and hand measurements, and check your span and the way your thumb lies in relation to your other fingers. He will then very carefully drill the first holes for your fingers. It is always possible to enlarge a finger hole that is too tight but most difficult to narrow one once drilled (usually the ball must be plugged with a filler and then redrilled; that is a nuisance and a disappointment).

So, patiently bear with your ball driller as he asks you to try out your ball to see how it works. Your thumb hole fit is most important. You dare not have it too loose or you will drop the ball too soon. You dare not have it too tight or binding for fear the ball will not come off your thumb at all—or much too late and cause a pull at the line.

You should be able to hold your ball with only your thumb in it. If you cannot do that, the hole is too large or else the ball is too heavy for you.

Your finger holes should not be fitted as tightly as your thumb. On the other hand, you do want the depth of the drilling exact, so that you can put your fingers in the holes in the same way, to the same depth, and with the same pressure every time. Your ball driller will work with you on this, drilling out a little more and then a little more until each fingertip just touches the bottom of the finger hole.

At first you should use the conventional three-finger drilling of the ball that your professional driller recommends. Then as you progress in the game and improve you will want to experiment with a *stronger* ball, one that hooks more at the end of its travel down the lane. The stronger finger drillings are called *semi-fingertip* and *fingertip*. The fingertip ball is drilled so that only the last joints of the third and fourth fingers are inserted into the ball. That widens the ball span an extra inch or so and allows the bowler to impart more action at the delivery point. With the wider span, too, the bowler is less likely to overturn the ball at delivery by letting his fingers get ahead of his thumb. The semi-fingertip drilling is a compromise between the first two drillings I have mentioned. In the *semi* the ball is carried on the pads of flesh between the second and third knuckles of the third and fourth fingers. The weight of the ball is spread more evenly into the whole hand on the semi than it is in the fingertip ball. Both semi-fingertip and fingertip drillings require considerable finger and hand strength in the bowler, so if you care to try these stronger balls you may have to increase your hand and finger strength to be successful with either one of them.

Since the true fingertip ball requires the most strength I suggest you experiment first with the semi, which requires less hand and finger strength than the fingertip drilling. Some of the exercises I recommend in Chapter 9 are meant to give you that necessary finger, hand, and wrist strength.

You must have not only the proper ball fit in your ball but also the proper ball balance. The American Bowling Congress is the czar of bowling and has set down the rules for bowling, the size and weight of pins, and the specifications for the lanes; it has also ordered bowling ball specifications which require the ball to be essentially in perfect balance as it rolls down the lane. However, it does permit slight imbalances to exist; for example, on the ball that weighs more than 10 pounds, "not more than three ounces difference between the top of the ball (the finger hole side) and the bottom of the ball (the solid side opposite the finger holes)" and also "not more than one ounce difference between the sides to the right and left of the finger holes or between the sides in front and back of the finger holes."

You may ask, "What does that mean to me?" I'll admit it sounds complicated, and it is. But the net effect of the slightest imbalance in the ball, although legally allowed by the American Bowling Congress rules, is that the roll of the ball is affected as it goes down the lanes. Sometimes the amount of hook will be greater with one type of imbalance. Sometimes the hitting power of the ball can be delayed until it occurs just as the ball reaches the pins. Once more, I tell you to trust your professional ball driller to drill for you the type of ball you need not only for finger fit but also for dynamic balance.

Another factor you and your expert will consider is, what kind of bowling ball will you buy and use? Today bowling balls are constructed in many different ways. Some are pure plastic, even clear enough to see through. Some are mixtures of rubber and plastic. Some have thin outer shells; some thicker ones. Some have porous outer coats; others are hard. The bowling fact is that the more porous the outer coating of a ball is, the more it grips the lane and hooks. The harder it is, the more it slides and its hooking action is delayed.

So in discussing this fourth fundamental of championship bowling, *correct ball fit and ball balance,* I trust that you now are aware of the myriad of possibilities open to you as a bowler looking for the right ball for you. As you will see in Chapter 14, "Special Tips for the High Average Bowler" I recommend that you consider having more than one bowling ball fitted and balanced for you. The constantly changing lane conditions of today, the new products being used in bowling ball manufacture, the new plastic coatings and different oils on the lanes, are all things that require the serious bowler of today to own and use more than one bowling ball if he hopes to become a championship bowler.

Incidentally, I own about 50 bowling balls myself and am still searching for the one I can use on certain lane conditions I encounter. Bowling is getting more complicated every day!

*Correct ball fit and ball balance are of the utmost importance to all bowlers.
Here I am in my own pro shop checking the balance of one of my "strong"
balls. A half ounce of weight shifted from one side of the ball to the other can
affect the final action of the ball at the pocket. It is necessary for every bowler
to have the confidence of an expert ball driller who can advise him on his ball
fit and ball balance.*

It may take you years to find the bowling ball that fits your game.
However, in order to become a champion bowler you must possess a
bowling ball with correct fit and balance.

One of the most famous ball drillers in the professional world today
is my good friend, Larry Lichstein. He is so good at drilling the "right"
ball for the pros that he travels around the professional bowlers circuit
in his own remodeled Greyhound bus—truly a "Ball Drilling and
Bowling Supply Motor Home." Larry claims that "ball drilling is an
art, not a science, and that the trick (for the ball driller) is to find the
reason why a bowler's ball does not work and make the necessary
correction to get the desired results." Lichstein believes, by the way,
that the ordinary bowler should have at least two balls drilled to fit him:

Here are three of my favorite balls. I call them my strong, stronger, *and* strongest *because each one is weighted in a slightly different way to give me more hook at the end of the lane—power in the pocket where I need it. I recommend that every bowler use three bowling balls of similar style. Consult your professional ball driller and let him prescribe for you!*

one of rubber composition, the other of plastic in order to help him conquer most of the hard conditions he will encounter.

A general rule, Larry says, is that top weight, finger weight, and right side weight in the ball will produce more hook; while bottom weight, thumb weight, and left side weight will tend to hold back the hooking action. So you might keep these thoughts in mind when you consult with your own ball drilling specialist.

APPLICATION OF SQUEEZE ACTION

The most important fundamental of championship bowling is the *squeeze,* the explosive finger action which the fingers impart to the ball at that fraction of a second when the ball begins to leave the bowler's hand and rotates to the left on its way down the lane to a powerful strike.

All the other fundamentals of bowling focus on this so-called explosion point of bowling. If the bowler's rhythm is faulty, if he is not square to his line, if he commits any fault in his swing before he delivers the ball, he never reaches the proper body attitude which will permit the explosive release by the fingers.

Now about the application of the squeeze at the explosion point: Not only must the fingers close sharply against the palm of the hand, but they must also close always on the same axis for the bowler to impart a consistent angle of rotation or lift on the ball. That is, the fingers in closing should not move from 5 o'clock to 11 o'clock on a clock dial one time and the next time from 4 o'clock to 10 o'clock or 3 o'clock to 9 o'clock. There must be consistency of the finger angle on the squeeze. The average bowler has to choose what finger angle he wants to use, but once the angle is chosen he should stay with that angle, not varying it. The high average bowler is an exception to this rule. In Chapter 14 on advice to the high average bowler we will discuss changing the finger angle.

Remember the most important fundamental of championship bowling: *Always release the ball with the explosive squeeze finger action!*

This is the imaginary clock dial that the bowler should visualize as he imparts the squeeze action at the delivery. He should see his fingers closing from 5 o'clock to 11 o'clock, from 4 o'clock to 10 o'clock, or from 3 o'clock to 9 o'clock. The closing action must be consistently the same in order to give the best results.

CONSISTENT WRIST ACTION AND FULL FOLLOW-THROUGH

Basically, there are two methods of releasing the ball at the foul line with a technique which leads to strong effective action on the ball. The first one, without turning the wrist, I consider to be the most natural ball, one that most beginning bowlers roll. In this delivery the bowler does not attempt to twist the ball at the last second of delivery. He merely lets the ball come off his thumb first, and then his fingers close on the ball in the squeeze action which puts power into the ball at the pins.

Using the natural *no wrist turn* release, the bowler takes the ball back in his backswing, being careful to keep his thumb on the inside; that is, on the side of the ball toward his body. In many examples of this no wrist turn delivery there can be seen a distinct counterclockwise turn of the ball as the ball passes the bowler's side in his downward backswing.

That counterclockwise turn should be no more than enough to keep the thumb in position on the side of the ball so that the fingers can remain under the ball, to the right, and behind the thumb. Remember that the wrist is not broken downward in any way but remains firm throughout the delivery. Try to visualize your thumb constantly pointing to a 10 o'clock position on a clock dial. If you really concentrate you can see your thumb in your mind's eye in that position all through your backswing and into your downswing.

Remember that it is most important that you do not let your fingers catch up to and pass your thumb at the last second as the ball comes off your hand. Your fingers *must* remain to the side, ready to squeeze forward on a 5 o'clock to 11 o'clock, a 4 o'clock to 10 o'clock, or even just short of a 3 o'clock to 9 o'clock delivery angle. (Note: Your squeezing fingers must not pass 3 o'clock on the side of the ball or you will have over-turned the ball and lost any chance of action.)

In this no wrist turn, or natural, release the ball comes forward as the bowler slides at the foul line. Because the bowler's thumb is shorter than the rest of his fingers, and also because of the bowler's reaching motion to put the ball out over the foul line, the thumb gets out of the ball before the fingers do and thus the fingers have their chance to stay in the ball a split second longer than the thumb, squeeze the ball, and lift the ball forward on target down the intended target line. Remember that in this type of natural delivery the bowler does not twist his wrist in a counterclockwise fashion at the moment of delivery. The bowler's arm and hand come straight up after they have released the ball.

Now, let's contrast the natural no wrist turn delivery with the second style of ball release, the delivery with wrist turn. The important fact about this second type of delivery is that the bowler must maneuver his hand and wrist during his backswing so that he can get his fingers and thumb into a position on the ball from which, at that last split second, he can give the ball the wrist turn motion he wants to impart.

So in order to do this, the bowler who uses wrist turn must, either early or late in his backswing, get his thumb turned to at least a 12 o'clock position on the ball with his fingers at a 6 o'clock position. In fact, in the deliveries of bowlers who are called *crankers,* the thumb may be twisted from a 10 o'clock, to a 6 o'clock position or even more drastic counterclockwise position before the bowler starts his downswing.

Basically, in order to use the wrist turn method, the bowler must keep his fingers well behind the ball as it comes forward in its downswing until a fraction of a second before the ball release. Then the fingers come from behind the ball as the wrist begins to turn counterclockwise (usually from a 12 o'clock–6 o'clock position to a 10 o'clock–4 o'clock position) and the fingers perform their squeeze action, lifting the ball forward and putting it on an axis toward 11 o'clock, 10 o'clock, or even close to 9 o'clock depending upon the exact plane on which the final release is made.

From my description of the two types of delivery I am sure you will agree that the first, the natural no wrist turn delivery, is simple and easier to do. In addition, since the bowler must maneuver his fingers and thumb through about 90 degrees of turn away from the line and then back to the line, there is the technical problem of performing this delicate maneuver in the same way every time. The great bowlers can do it, but only after thousands of hours of practice.

I recommend that most of my readers attempt to perfect the natural no wrist turn delivery. On the other hand, some bowlers seem to perform the *wrist turn* delivery as their natural delivery. If that is true in your case then obviously you should stay with that method and try to perfect it. Both methods work in producing an explosive bowling ball. The ball delivery with wrist turn usually has more hooking action and therefore crosses more boards on its way to the pocket. When a bowling ball has to cross a number of boards in its track it is more subject to the influence of irregularities in the lane. The rule in general is that the more boards you cross, the more trouble you get into. So in many cases there is a trade-off by the bowler who rolls a ball with strong wrist turn. In return for the danger he encounters when he crosses the boards he often picks up a more powerful ball with greater drive at the pocket.

We all must work with the equipment we possess: our natural body strength, our natural athletic ability and coordination, the sizes and shapes of our fingers, even our various desires to excel at sport. My best advice to you is to roll the ball that comes most naturally to you and you are bound to succeed.

I would like to emphasize the importance of your making a full, strong follow-through at the foul line with your body leaning well forward as you release the ball. In order for you to be able to squeeze the ball at the delivery point it is absolutely necessary that your hand, your arm, your shoulder, your entire body must follow through down your target line as long as the ball remains in your hand, and then for a few seconds more after the ball is gone on its way. And that follow-through must be straight up, not to the side by a single degree. Straight up and through!

So often I see bowlers snap the ball at the line, withdrawing their fingers almost as if they can't wait to get rid of it. Other bowlers let their hands and wrists go limp at the delivery point and thus have no chance to put action on the ball.

Not only must the squeeze finger action be used as the ball comes off the fingers at the explosion point, but the bowler's body, his hand, and his arm must stay with the ball as long as possible down the target line in order to develop a consistent bowling champion's style.

I would like you to observe the best modern baseball pitchers. See how the pitcher's arm comes through and down his target line as he pitches to the plate. His follow-through is just as important as yours is. If necessary I want you to exaggerate your bowling follow-through. As you practice your bowling you can keep track of your finishing hand and arm position as the ball makes its way to the pins. I recommend that you practice holding your finish on every delivery in practice to check two things: First, that your sliding foot is straight down your target line, and second, that you have followed straight through with your hand and arm. The famous bowler, Ned Day, would often be seen stopped at the line and with his hand well through the ball and up over his left shoulder. He said that when he could see his hand in that position he knew he had followed through correctly.

SPEED CONTROL

The *seventh* fundamental of championship bowling is *speed control*.

Speed refers to the time it takes your bowling ball to go from the point of release at the foul line to the headpin. The average speed of a professional bowler is approximately 2.5 seconds. Some good bowlers roll a faster ball, some a slower one, but in general your ball speed should range from 2.1 seconds to 2.8 seconds. You should arrange to have some friend time your ball speed with a stop watch so you will know where you stand in relation to the professionals.

Ball speed is one of the most difficult factors for every bowler, professional or amateur, to control. Remember that the faster a ball is rolled, the more it will deflect as it moves by the head pin. Think of a car skidding on an icy pavement. The faster it goes, the less traction or "bite" it has.

The slower a ball is thrown, the more hook it will have. This is true in

Here is a demonstration of a bowling delivery with the ball held at about chest height. I personally favor this style because I believe it gives me the speed of delivery I want. Every bowler must find his own way to do it. This is a good way; you might try it.

This picture demonstrates the start of the delivery at waist height, close to the body. It is an excellent method for the beginner to use as it allows him to synchronize his first step with his pushaway in the delivery. Later on he can adjust this starting position upward or downward when he wants more or less speed.

general, but on the other hand, when it is rolling slower it may exhaust its power by the time it reaches the pocket.

Here are three ways to change speed. First, the most popular way and easiest: change the height of your pushaway. If you start your pushaway from a higher position, your backswing will also be higher and your ball speed will be increased. You will need to walk a little slower to the line in order to compensate for the greater length of time to complete your armswing.

The second way to change speed is to adjust the length of your approach. The closer you stand to the foul line the slower the ball speed with all other factors the same. The farther back you stand, the more speed you will get.

The third way is to *muscle* the ball; that is, exert more power physically at the point of release. It is hard to do this and do it smoothly. Furthermore, when the bowler muscles the ball he may not impart the same action as he does when he delivers his normal nonspeeded ball. The ball may lose carrying power as a result.

Another factor which must be taken into consideration is the length of the track of the ball down the lane. Putting the ball down an inch beyond the foul line and lofting it out 12 to 14 inches are entirely two different matters. The first ball may begin to hook before it gets to the pocket, while the second ball may hook too late and miss the pocket.

As I have remarked, *speed control* is the most difficult fundamental of all to perfect. You will achieve it only through hours and hours of practice. To be a champion bowler you must have speed control.

4
THE FOUR
GROUPS FOR
SPARE SHOOTING

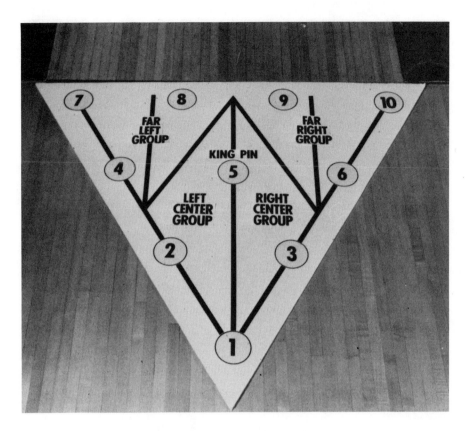

The Four Groups for Spare Shooting

Here is a simple diagram of the various groupings that control your starting position in order to convert spares and many splits. You should study it and memorize it! The 4-7-8 constitutes the Far Left Group, the 6-9-10 the Far Right Group. Reverse the name of the group and, in general, you have your starting position: Far Left—Far Right Starting Position, and vice versa. In the center of the alley is the Left Center Group that has the 1-2-5-8 pins, and the Right Center Group with the 1-3-5-9 pins. The presence or absence of the 5-pin makes a difference in your starting position to convert the Left or Right Center Group spares. Left Center Group spares, in general, are bowled from Right Center Starting Position and Right Center Group spares from Left Center Starting Position.

The Left Center Group (with the 5-Pin)

The 1-2-5-8 constitutes the Left Center Group and is bowled from Strike Position over your normal strike line right into the 1-3 pocket. This cluster might just as well be an entire setup of ten pins. The 5-pin is the controlling factor here and the ball must be rolled with your usual explosive finger action so that the 5-pin will be taken out. If you should happen to have either the 4-pin or the 7-pin (or both) added to the Left Center Group you will still bowl from the Strike Position, inasmuch as the Center Group's importance and position control your decision.

The Left Center Group (without the 5-Pin)

The 1–2–8 group constitutes the Left Center Group (without the 5-pin) and should be bowled from Strike Position, Brooklyn Line. *By this expression, I mean that you start from your normal strike position with your left toe on the center spot; but by picking out one board left of your strike board or strike line at the break of the boards (which you can see in the following picture), your ball will travel across the lane into the 1–2 pocket and will take the 8-pin out on its way through. The addition of the 4- or 7-pin makes no difference to this setup. Always bowl from Strike Position, Brooklyn Line.*

The Right Center Group

The 1–3–5–9 constitutes the Right Center Group, and you will use Left Center Starting Position to convert these pins or nearly any combination of them. If you have pins added from the Far Right Group such as the 6-pin or the 10-pin (or perhaps both), your best strategy is to remain in Left Center Starting Position in order to decrease your chances of cutting off one or more of the pins. If the 5-pin is present, experiment to find whether it is easier for you to convert the Right Center Group spares from Strike Position or from Left Center. But once you find out your best way, stay with it from then on—don't vary.

The Far Right Group

The 6-, 9-, and 10-pins are in the Far Right Group. Always bowl for them from Far Left Starting Position. The only exception to this is that you may find you can make the 9-pin alone from the Left Center Position, since it is also a part of that group. But if you have the 6-pin standing with either the 9-pin or the 10-pin you have a better angle, and therefore a better chance to convert, by rolling from the Far Left Starting Position. In practice, you should make this spare alternately by hitting first the 6–10 pocket and then the 6–9 pocket.

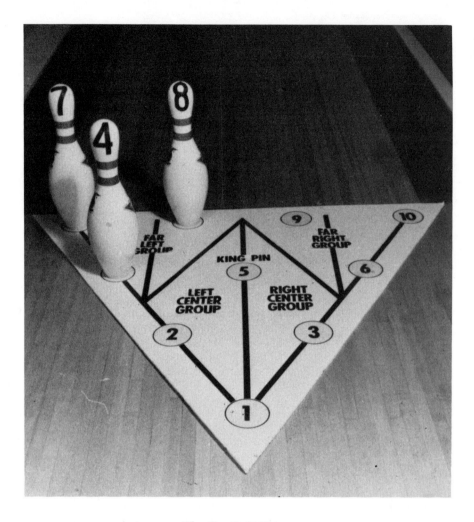

The Far Left Group

The 4-, 7-, and 8-pins are in the Far Left Group and should almost without exception be bowled from Far Right Starting Position. Remember: To allow for the extra distance the ball must travel to get into the third or back row of pins, you must choose a line or spot slightly to the right of the line your eye tells you to use. Most spares in the back row of pins are missed on the left-hand side because of the failure to make this allowance.

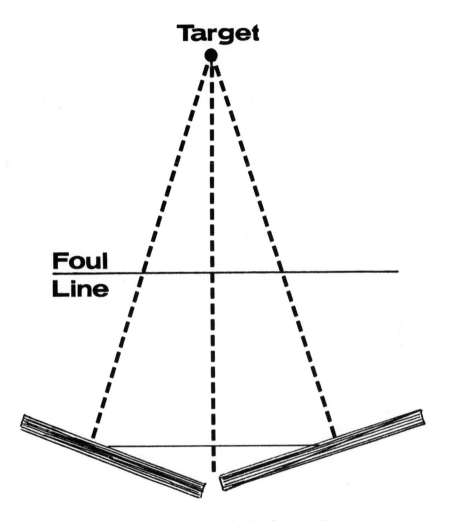

Far Left and Far Right Bowling Angles

The dotted lines on the right and left in this drawing indicate the cross-lane angle that results from your starting from Far Right Starting Position or from Far Left Starting Position. The center line represents your normal angle, square to the line. It is this angling for your spare that takes advantage of the width of the ball track to help you to knock down the greatest number of pins.

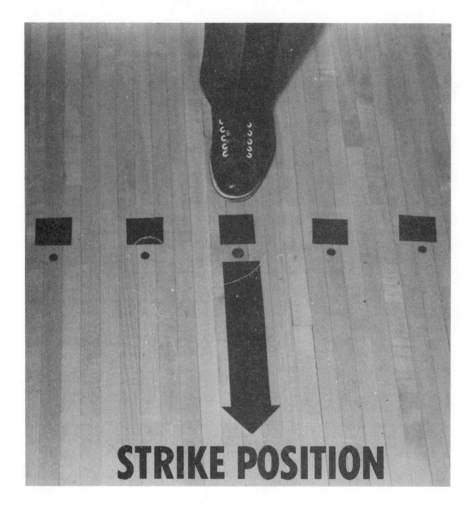

Strike Position

For your starting position for a strike hit in the 1–3 pocket, place your left foot on the center dot and your right shoulder in line with your strike line, board, or spot. For the Left Center Group (with the 5-pin), always bowl from your natural Strike Position, primarily because of the presence of the 5-pin. Since it is the kingpin and hard to get out of the cluster, your strike angle is the best one to use.

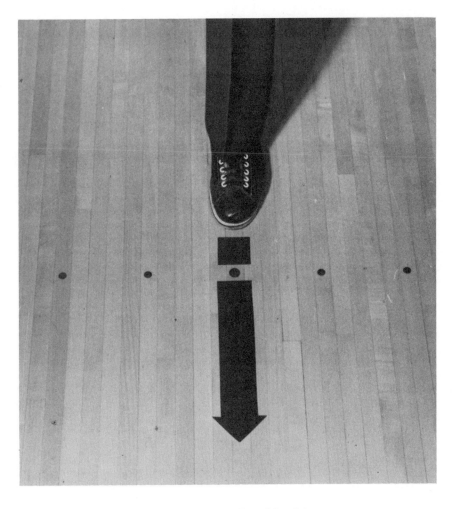

Strike Position, Brooklyn Line

You remain in your normal Strike Position with your left foot on the center dot. But this time you aim one board left of your normal strike spot at the break of the boards. Your ball will travel from six to eight inches left of your usual strike line. The result is that it will come in on the 1–2 or Brooklyn pocket in very much the same manner that it would have come into the 1–3 pocket if you had not aimed the single board left.

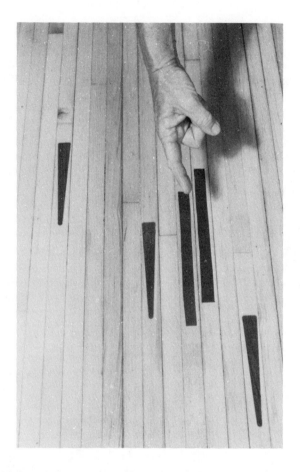

How to Choose Your Board or Line for Strike Position, Brooklyn Line

I have applied two black lines to the lane between the second and third dart indicators from the right. The black line on the right represents your normal spot, board, or line that takes your ball into the 1-3 strike pocket. The line on the board to its left shows the line that the ball must travel in order to cross over the headpin and hit the 1-2 pocket for a Brooklyn hit. You do not change your starting position. Your ball will travel one board left of its usual strike line, and the slight resulting angle does the work of bringing it into the 1-2 pocket.

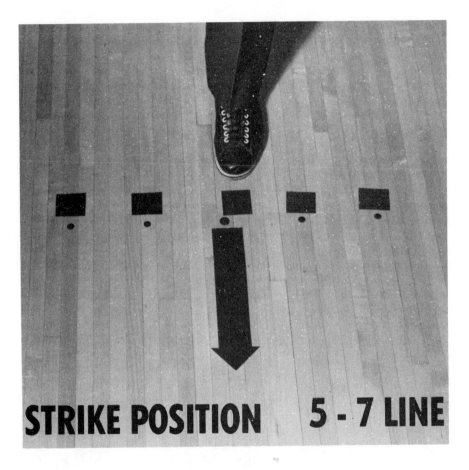

Strike Position, 5–7 Line

Look carefully at this photo and compare it with the photo of the normal strike position. The target foot is moved one board left of its normal position and the ball will be rolled over the strike spot at the break of the boards. This line causes the ball to come in light on the 5-pin and will cause the 5-pin to be driven over to take out the 7-pin.

Right Center Starting Position

Place your target foot on the fifth board to the right of the center dot. Bowling from this angle will clear all the spares in the Left Center Group.

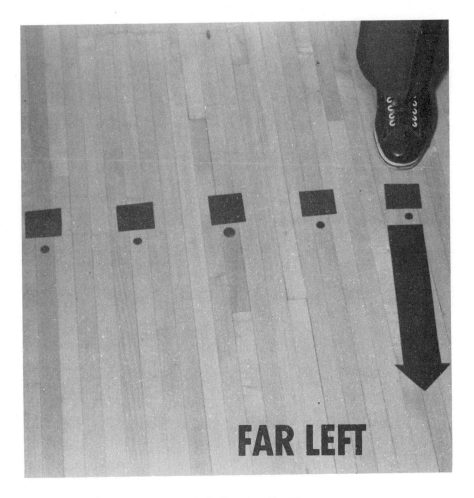

Far Left Starting Position

Place your left foot on the fourteenth board left of your center or strike dot. Square yourself directly toward the pins on the far right side of the lane. Your approach will be directly toward the pins and definitely cross-alley. However, be aware of the fact that, since your ball will be delivered from the right-hand side of your body, your actual delivery point at the foul line will be at about the middle of the alley. Follow through directly toward the pins and do not ease up in any manner. Use Far Left Starting Position for Far Right Group spares.

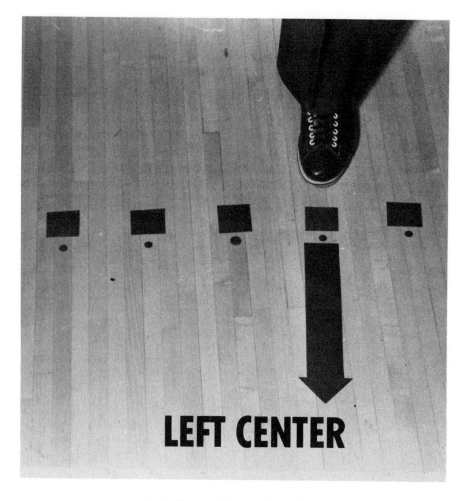

Left Center Starting Position

Place your left foot on the seventh board left of the center dot and square yourself toward the pins and your spare, just as if you are rolling a first ball. You will be delivering this ball slightly across the lane. This starting position is used for Right Center Group pins. If your spare has pins in both Right Center Group and Far Right Group, the importance of getting the Right Center Group pins determines your starting position and controls your start from Left Center.

Far Right Starting Position

Place your left foot on the fourteenth board to the right of the center dot and square yourself directly toward the pins in the Far Left Group. If the 8-pin is standing alone, you may prefer to bowl from Strike Position, Brooklyn Line, but in general if you have the 4-pin alone, the 7-pin alone, or both 4-pin and 7-pin, you are better off to use the entire width of the alley in angling for your spare. You will miss less often if you do.

5
HOW
TO MAKE
YOUR SPARES

Dawson Taylor, five-time Detroit Athletic Club Champion, smiles as he realizes that with his average of 200 pins he will be Captain of the D.A.C. Inter-Club team once more.

The magic of attaining a high average in bowling lies in converting as many spares as possible. No bowler can strike in every frame. In order to maintain a 200 average—a very good one we will all agree—it is only necessary to average four strikes per game with no more than two open frames in each three-game series.

So, mathematically speaking, the good bowler needs to convert 18 frames of spares in every three-game series in order to maintain a 200 average.

In the following pages you will find a careful analysis of the various starting positions and their corresponding targets at the darts or arrows at the break of the boards or splice. With intelligent application and study you will become familiar with every normal spare and all the frequent split combinations. You will learn how to convert every one of them!

LEFT-HAND SPARES

The 2-Pin Spare, Left Center Group
Starting Position: Strike Position, Brooklyn Line

You should be able to bowl this spare with your eyes closed. You have practiced and practiced on your Strike Position start that brings your ball into the 1–3 pocket and on your Strike Position, Brooklyn Line that brings your ball into the 1–2 pocket. Remember that you have a target area of 23 inches to hit and be sure that you hit it. Use this single pin for practice on your 1–2 pocket hit and for making the imaginary 1–2–10 washout. *Picture the 8-pin back of it and work on making that* tandem *or* sleeper *leave. Watch where the ball goes to make sure it would have taken out the imaginary 8-pin!*

The 1–2–10 Washout Spare
Starting Position: Strike Position, Brooklyn Line

You should be able to convert this troublesome spare without too much difficulty. It usually results from a ball that is pitched too far out on the lane and consequently begins to act too late and gets behind the headpin. It also indicates a flat ball, or one without proper finger action. On your spare be sure that you keep your thumb to the left and that you have the explosive finger action, and the headpin will be snapped over and across the alley to take out the 10-pin. The headpin must be struck flush on its left side to direct it at the 10-pin.

The 1-2-8 Spare, Left Center Group
Starting Position: Strike Position, Brooklyn Line

This spare, the 1-2, the 1-2-4-8, the 1-2-4-7, and the delightful 1-2-10 washout are all bowled in exactly the same manner, from Strike Position, Brooklyn Line. Since you are in your familiar starting position you should be more relaxed than usual. It is not difficult to hit that board to the left of your strike pin, and if you do you will carry through to take out the 8-pin with your strong ball. Don't fail to give your ball the necessary explosive finger action at release, for you must have as much action on this (or the other-named spares) as you need on your first ball to strike.

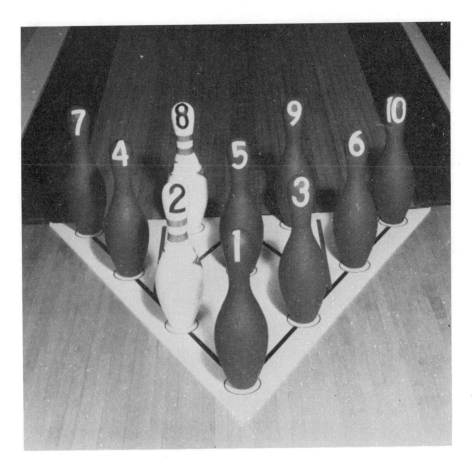

The 2–8 Spare, Left Center Group
Starting Position: Strike Position, Brooklyn Line

Now that you have been practicing on the 1–2 pocket from Strike Position, Brooklyn Line, you have the opportunity to prove that you can hit it with authority. The 2-pin must be hit on the right-hand side and the ball must have enough power of its own to overcome its tendency to deflect away from the 8-pin. The ball will take out the 8-pin. Sometimes you may miss your target and still get the break of having the 2-pin fly back to take out the 8-pin. Don't count on it! The distance is the same 22 inches that the 5-pin is away from the headpin, and your chances that it will happen are remote.

The 2–4–5–8 Spare, Left Center Group
Starting Position: Right Center

Imagine that you have a baby strike setup and plan to hit firmly in the 2–5 pocket as if it were the 1–3 of a full setup. You have to rely on the 2-pin taking out the 4-pin and so your hit has to be high on the 2-pin. This is a hateful spare and a much dreaded one. Be sure to concentrate on your finger action because your ball must have "stuff" on it to help it get through to the 8-pin. If you miss your pocket and come in on the left side, you may still be lucky enough to convert it by having the 2-pin get the 5-pin and the ball take the 8-pin away. Practice on this spare a great deal and you will lose your fear of it.

The 2-4-8 Spare, Left Center Group
Starting Position: Strike Position, Brooklyn Line

This spare is a blood brother to the nasty 2-4-5-8 spare just discussed. It is a little easier because the 5-pin is gone, but don't fail to work hard on converting it. Come in high on the 2-pin so as to deflect it into the 4-pin, and be sure that the ball has the action to carry through to take out the 8-pin. You can't make this spare very often if you hit in the 2-4 pocket because the ball will deflect away from the 8-pin and leave it standing. If you leave the 8-pin you have left your "mother-in-law"! This is another one of those spares it is better not to leave.

The 2–4–5 Spare, Left Center Group
Starting Position: Strike Position, Brooklyn Line

This spare results from a very thin hit on the right side of the headpin. Since there are three pins, it is a difficult spare and it is easy to cherrypick either the 4-pin or the 5-pin. The best way to make it is to bowl from Strike Position, Brooklyn Line so as to come into the 2–5 pocket strongly enough to cause the 2-pin to go back into the 4-pin and take it out while the ball takes the 5-pin. This strategy is good, too, in case you pull your ball left, which you might do, for then you may still hit in the 2–4 pocket and still get the 5-pin with the 2-pin. The best advice on this spare is, "Don't leave it!"

The 2–5 Spare, Left Center Group
Starting Position: The One You Find Best for You

This is an exception to the rule on groupings. For the reason that a curving ball is apt to cut off the front pin of these two, most good bowlers move to their left and shoot at this spare from either head-on or even slightly left of head-on in order to cut down the chop angle and make the ball track take care of the back pin. Try all the positions on this spare, and once you find one that helps you to cover them regularly, stay with it. Try bowling at the 5-pin alone or at the 2-pin alone, and forgetting that the other is up. It may help.

The 1-2-4-7 Spare, Left Center Group
Starting Position: Strike Position, Brooklyn Line

This spare is known as the clothesline *or* fence post. *Any time you leave more than one pin in a spare you are in danger of missing. So here your danger is quadrupled. You must have the help of the 4-pin to take out the 7-pin after your ball has hit into the Brooklyn 1-2 pocket. Your ball must have action in order to deflect as far as the 4-pin, so be certain that you apply the squeeze. If you move too far right to make this spare you will find that you may miss the headpin. Any way you shoot for it, it is a very difficult spare and quite a pleasure to convert.*

The 7-Pin Spare, Far Left Group
Starting Position: Far Right

Although this pin is similar to the 10-pin in that it is a smaller target than usual because it is so close to the channel, it is not as difficult to knock down as the 10-pin, because your ball is curving into it rather than away from it. Don't ever loaf on a 7- or 10-pin, or you will find yourself missing the pin on the left. Sometimes, too, by loafing you may forget to give your ball the necessary finger action at release and it may die short of the pin and miss on the right. Be careful, line yourself up facing the pin, and walk directly toward the 7-pin. Try to hit it squarely, or at least on the right side, and you won't miss it very often.

The 4-7 Spare, Far Left Group
Starting Position: Far Right

This spare is so easy that you must be careful not to be too casual about it. Bowl from Far Right Position and don't forget to give your ball the explosive finger action as you release it. If your ball flattens—and this is possible for it has to travel three feet or so farther—it might catch the 4-pin on its right side so thin that the 4-pin wraps around the 7-pin. You should never miss this spare on the left-hand side. If you do, it indicates that you have loafed and lost your speed. If you want to, practice on the imaginary 4-7-10 split and slide the 4-pin over to take out the imaginary 10-pin. In league play, however, don't experiment. Get your two-pin count every time.

The 2–4–7 Spare, Far Left Group
Starting Position: Far Right

Plan to hit the 2-pin on its left side, and the ball will deflect into the 4-pin and possibly all the way to the 7-pin. If not, the 4-pin may take the 7-pin out. If you come in too directly on the 4-pin, you may hit it too far on its right side, wrap it around the 7-pin, and miss it. This spare is not too difficult because your ball will be curving into the pins. Once in a while it is made on the outside by striking the 2-pin on its right side and letting the pins take each other out. It is not the safe way to do it, although you may get away with it. Better to hit all three pins with the ball, if you can!

RIGHT-HAND SPARES

The 3–5–6–9 Spare
Starting Position: Left Center

This is the left-hander's "bucket," and is one of the most difficult spares for either a left-hander or right-hander to make. Bowl from Left Center and imagine that the cluster is a miniature full setup. Try to hit the 3–6 pocket with lots of action so as to carry through and get the 9-pin. This is often cherried, so don't be upset when it happens to you. It happens to the best of us!

The 3–6–9 Spare, Right Center Group
Starting Position: Left Center

It is very easy to pick a cherry on this spare, so be careful not to move too far left. If you do, your ball may take out the 3- and 6-pins and leave the 9-pin standing. By bowling from Left Center, your ball can come in high and hard on the 3- and 9-pins, and the 3-pin will either go back and take out the 9-pin while the ball takes the 6-pin, or the ball will knock the 3-pin to its left and go through and take out both 6- and 9-pins. Practice on this spare so you can cover the 3- and 9-pins and you will rarely leave the 6-pin standing.

The 5-9 Spare, Right Center Group
Starting Position: Left Center

This leave very often occurs on a Brooklyn or 1-2 pocket hit where the ball goes to the left of the headpin. It is a hard spare because of your chance to pick a cherry out of either pin. By bowling from Left Center Starting Position you will have the best angle to make this spare. Be sure to roll the ball a little faster because the pins are farther back than usual. If you find that you are sliding by the 5-pin and taking the 9-pin out on the right side, move a little to your right until you find that you are getting the 5-pin and leaving the 9-pin. Everybody chops this once in a while, so don't worry too much if you do, too!

The 3–9 Spare, Right Center Group
Starting Position: Left Center

This is a mean tandem spare that happens when the bowler misses the headpin on the left side. It has to be hit absolutely dead on, and the ball cannot deflect at all or else the "mother-in-law" in the back row will remain standing. I recommend a little extra speed on this spare to cut down on deflection. This spare is as hard to convert as a wide-open split. It is a tough one!

The 1–3–6–10 Spare, Right Center Group
Starting Position: Far Left or Left Center

The fact that you have the 1- and 3-pins in this wicked leave controls your strategy as to whether to bowl this from Far Left or Left Center. Your ball must hit in the 1–3 pocket and get some help from the 6-pin in taking out the 10-pin. If you move too far left in an attempt to cover them all you may slide by the headpin. Once in a while this can be made on the outside, clipping the headpin on its left side, but your probabilities are much more remote than they are by using the ball to do some of the work. It's a hard spare, especially for a strong curve ball that is breaking away from the pins. Don't be too upset if you miss it. The bowler with a strong breaking curve should use the Far Left Starting Position; the bowler with a weaker ball the Left Center Starting Position.

The 6–10 Spare, Far Right Group
Starting Position: Far Left

This spare, along with the 5–9 and the 2–5 spares, is difficult for the right-handed bowler with a strong hook because of the tendency of the hook to cut sharply through the front pin and cut it off from the pin to the right. You may find that you can lessen the number of your chops by aiming for the pin to the right and trying to hit it full, using as much angle as you can. In general, the more angle, the less the chance for the cherry pick. Roll for the 6–10 from Far Left Starting Position. Your ball will usually come up the inch or so necessary to take out the front pin.

The 10-Pin Spare, Far Right Group
Starting Position: Far Left

Since this pin is in the back row and because of the tendency of your ball to run left at the last moment, you must throw harder at the 10-pin to cover it. Be sure that you square your body to the pin and walk directly toward it. You must follow through on this pin especially, because if you loaf you will be sure to see your ball take off at the end of its track and miss the pin on the left side. Some bowlers picture a pin standing in the gutter to the right and aim for it. Always try to hit the 10-pin flush. This picture will help you to convert the 6-10 spare when you have it.

The 6-9-10 Spare, Far Right Group
Starting Position: Far Left

Pretend this is a baby strike and aim for the right-hand pocket. Forget about the 9-pin as you will probably get it with the 6-pin while the ball takes out the 10-pin. If you pull your ball a little left, or if it runs farther left than you wanted it to do, you may still make the spare on the outside, in the 6–9 pocket. If you always shoot for the right-hand pocket of this spare you will give yourself two chances of making it: the right way and the lucky way.

The 3-6-10 Spare, Far Right Group
Starting Position: Far Left

Play this spare as a baby strike, remembering that the cluster is several feet farther away and that your ball will be running left at the end of its track. Try to hit this spare solidly in the 3-6 pocket and the 6-pin will go on to take out the 10-pin even if the ball hooks through too far to the left. The more you can angle at this spare the more your hope of carrying all three pins with the ball, an ideal situation. Any time you hit all the pins of a spare with your ball you inevitably make it. This spare, obviously, is great for practice in making the 3-10 baby split.

The *1-3-5-8-9-10 Spare, the* Polish Cathedral
Starting Position: Left Center

This spare is a rarity, fortunately, and happens when the bowler misses the headpin on the left side with a ball going away from the cluster. It is called the Polish Cathedral *and in the history of bowling is known to have been converted only a few times. No matter what angle you use it seems that one pin will remain standing. Try Left Center for your best chance. It is said that if anyone in a Chicago league makes this spare he gets an audience with the Pope!*

6
SPLITS: THE PROBLEM—AND HOW TO CAPITALIZE ON THEM

A split is a leave of two or more pins with the head pin down and a gap of at least one pin between any other two pins. It is the fact that there is a missing pin which makes it so difficult to convert or make the split.

You will find out by experience, or you already know, that there are small splits (they're called baby splits), moderately wide splits, and wide-open splits. Wide-open splits are always those with two pins or more on opposite sides of the leave and in the same row, either the third row or the back row. These are so difficult to convert that they are usually called the *impossible* splits. But once in a while someone does convert an impossible split by great luck and sometimes skill. The American Bowling Congress awards a special arm patch for the shirt of anyone accurate enough, or lucky enough, to convert the "big four": the 4-6-7-10 split. Sometimes you will see the 4-7, the 8-10, or the 7-9 made when a bowler bounces one pin up into the rack or the padding in the pit and in ricochets back into the lane to clear the other pin.

Splits can be classified into three types, namely the *impossible,* the *fit-it-in-between,* and the *slide-it-over* splits. If you have left the 4–6 split on the third row, the 8–10 or the 7–9 in the back row, or the double combination of the 4–6, 7–10 in both the third and back row you have one of the impossibles. Let's consider these impossible splits and decide what to do about them when they occur.

Just why are these splits considered *impossible*? Because, since two of the pins are on the same line with each other, no matter what angle the ball strikes one of the pins, it is practically impossible to drive it over at an angle accurate enough to take out the other pin. Rarely, this does happen when a pin flies into the kickbacks or sideboards and rebounds into the lane to take out the remaining pin in the split. However, it is best not to plan on such an unlikely occurrence. Try to knock down as many pins in an impossible split as you can. If you get the 4–6–7–10 you can and should try to get three pins out of the leave. You will see how to do this in our discussion of how to convert the 4–7–10 or the 6–7–10 splits, two of the slide-it-over splits.

The *slide-it-over* splits are splits which are apparently wide-open at first glance and seem to be impossible but are in actuality possible because one pin is in the row of pins in front of the other or others. The slide-it-over splits can be made by bowling at the front pin in such a way as to slide it over against the other pins and thus convert or make the split. Examples of such splits are the 6–7–10 and the 4–7–10.

The *fit-it-in-between* splits, as the name implies, are those that can be made by bowling at the space between the pins, striking one to the right and one to the left of the ball as it fits in between the pins. Examples of fit-it-in-between splits are the 4–5, the 5–6, and the 9–10 splits.

Obviously, the object of bowling is for the bowler to attain as high a score as he possibly can. I am constantly amazed when I see bowlers throw away pins needlessly when they are shooting for splits or large spare groups.

It is useful for you to consider the various situations which can affect your score favorably and unfavorably and understand the strategy which should be employed when you encounter them.

Most important is deciding how to bowl against splits. In general, my advice for you is that if you have one of the so-called impossible splits, always try to get the greatest count you can. Incidentally, although some splits are called impossible to make, they can be made and many times have been made over the years by thousands of bowlers. The impossible splits are converted as a result of the bowling ball just barely touching one pin on its extreme right or left edge with enough side force to send it over on the same line of pins to the other pin of the split and hit it hard enough to topple it. Impossible splits are sometimes made by a freak bounce of the pins off the equipment so that an 8-pin or a 10-pin comes back from the pit to take out the other pin or pins in a wide open split. I myself once lost an important match in the last frame when my opponent converted an 8–10 unexpectedly that way. So don't ever count on your opponent not converting a split until after he has rolled at it and missed it.

Study the following diagrams and pictures and learn to recognize the splits which are impossible and those which can be made with skill (and luck!), and your bowling enjoyment will increase immeasurably.

The Fit-It-in-Between Splits

You can see in the picture above that you have about 2 inches more in ball width than the distance between the two pins—the 5–6, 4–5, 7–8, or 9–10. So these splits, along with the two baby splits—the 3–10 and the 2–7—are possible to convert by fitting the ball between the pins, hitting each pin, and knocking them both down. You can convert these splits regularly. And they're fun to make!

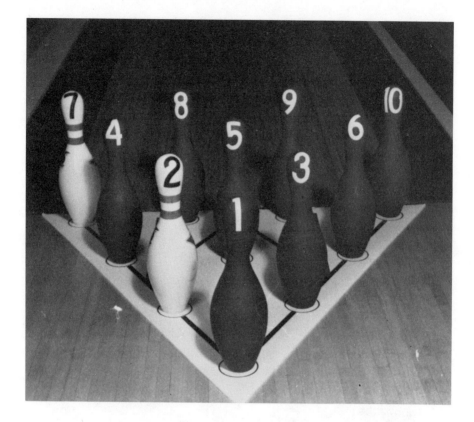

The 2–7 Fit-It-in-Between Split
Starting Position: Far Right

You can either shoot for the ghost 4-pin between the 2- and the 7-pins or for the left side of the 2-pin, but you will find that this baby split can be converted quite often. It is easier than the opposite 3–10 because your ball will be curving in toward the 7-pin and helping you to make it. Practice on this split and on the right-hand 3–10 baby split and you should convert them with regularity.

The 3–10 Fit-It-in-Between Split
Starting Position: Far Left

Bowl from Far Left Position. There are several different mental approaches to this split. Some bowlers shoot for the 10-pin and trust that the curve of the ball will bring it in on the right side of the 3-pin and that the deflection of the ball will take out the 10-pin. Another trick is to imagine the missing 6-pin and shoot to hit it dead on. Still another method is to roll the ball either directly for, or slightly to the left of, the particular spot at the break of the boards, which results in a 10-pin conversion for you. In practice, try making this split on the outside by hitting the 3-pin flush on its left side in order to throw it into the 10-pin. Then try it through the 6-pin slot. Experiment with all these methods and find the best way for you.

The 4–5 Fit-It-in-Between Split
Starting Position: Strike Position, Brooklyn Line

You can fit your ball between these two pins. This split is usually missed on the left because the bowler forgets that the pins are farther away in the third row, 22 inches beyond the headpin. So be sure to overallow to the right and you may have a better chance to make the split. Another trick is to imagine the missing 8-pin and shoot for it, forgetting about the two in front of it. Sometimes this works because it is relaxing to think of a spare rather than a split.

The 5-6 Fit-It-in-Between Split
Starting Position: Left Center

Bowl this split from Left Center Position. It usually results from a cross-over type of hit, going away from the headpin on the left. It is a harder split than the similar 4–5 split because you have to move from your normal starting position and because your ball will be traveling a line not frequently used and consequently of unknown characteristics. Be sure to allow a little more to the right than your eye tells you, as the pins are in the third row and your ball will be taking off in its curve in the last foot or so of its travel.

The Slide-It-Over Splits

As you can see from the illustration above and from the photographs that follow, if one of the pins is in the line in front of the others, even though the split is wide open it is not only possible but entirely practicable to convert this type of split. This is done by striking the pin in the front line at the proper angle so as to clip it over across the alley to take out the remaining pin. Your practice on the 10-pin and on the 4- and 6-pins will help you to make the slide-it-over splits often—and there is no greater thrill in bowling, let me assure you!

The 5–7 Slide-It-Over Split
Starting Position: Target Foot One Board Left of Strike Position

There is a trick to making this split and once you learn it, you will find that you will convert it often. As you remember, bowling from Strike Position to the board or left of your normal strike line brings you into the 1–2 pocket and results in what we call Strike Position, Brooklyn Line. If you move just one board left of your strike starting position with your left foot, and roll your ball over your strike line or strike spot at the break of the boards, your ball will be coming in sharply on the right-hand side of the 5-pin and you can snap it over smartly to take out the 7-pin. Practice hard on this and you can make it one out of three times!

The 5–10 Slide-It-Over Split
Starting Position: Strike Position, Brooklyn Line

This split is like the 8–10 split: an indicator of a weak ball, one that has failed to get in to the 5-pin, has flattened, and has died in the pocket. If you get this split or the 8–10 quite often, you are not using the proper finger action. Get back to fundamentals; roll the ball, making sure your thumb is out first and that you are imparting the proper explosive finger action at the delivery point. Make the 5–10 from Strike Position, Brooklyn Line. If you find it hard to make from this position, try moving a little left—it may work better for you. Experiment. Find your best angle and then stay with it until you are forced to change.

The 4-7-9 Slide-It-Over Split
Starting Position: Far Right

This split happens when you have a high hit on the headpin. It indicates that you should adjust your angle to come in more toward the 3-pin. Roll from Far Right Position and aim at the 7-pin alone. Shave the 4-pin on its left-hand side and you will clip it over to take out the 9-pin. This split is easier to make than the 4-7-10 because the 9-pin is a foot closer than the 10-pin. Sometimes it helps to pretend that you don't have the 9-pin standing and bowl for a thin 4-7 conversion. You can make it!

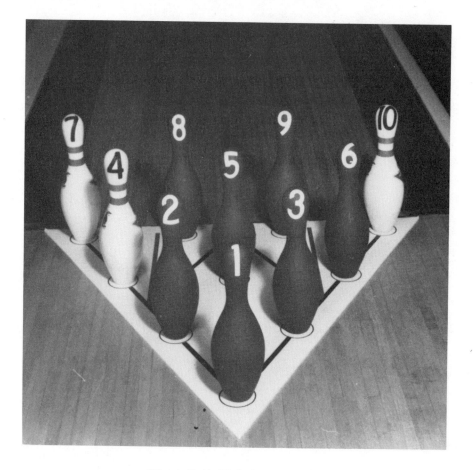

The 4–7–10 Slide-It-Over Split
Starting Position: Far Right

Plan to clip the 4-pin on its left side so as to slide it over and take out the 10-pin. The 4-pin must be hit extremely thin. This split is much more difficult to make than the reverse split—the 6–7–10—because your ball is going away from the 4-pin. I suggest that you aim for the 7-pin and forget about the 4-pin when you attempt to convert this split. If you make a thin hit on the 7-pin you will automatically catch the 4-pin thin enough to slide it over and take out the 10-pin. In league competition, don't try to make it unless it is urgently needed. Get the two pins on the left side and take advantage of your count.

The 6–7–10 Slide-It-Over Split
Starting Position: Far Left

Roll directly for the 10-pin. Try to hit the 10-pin on its right side, even with the idea of missing the 6-pin. The result will be that your ball will be coming in strongly on the right-hand side of the 6-pin and will snap it over sharply to take out the 7-pin. A slow ball or one that just touches the 6-pin often will cause it to slide over either in front of the 7-pin or so slowly that it will knock it down. That is most discouraging. Use good speed on this conversion and you will have a better chance to make it.

The 6-7-9-10 Slide-It-Over Split
Starting Position: Far Left

This is another wide-open split but is more easily converted than the 6-7-10 because, as a result of deflection, you may be able to get a favorable bounce of the 6-pin off the 9-pin more directly at the 7-pin. Try to hit the 6-pin lightly on its right side and you may make a spectacular conversion!

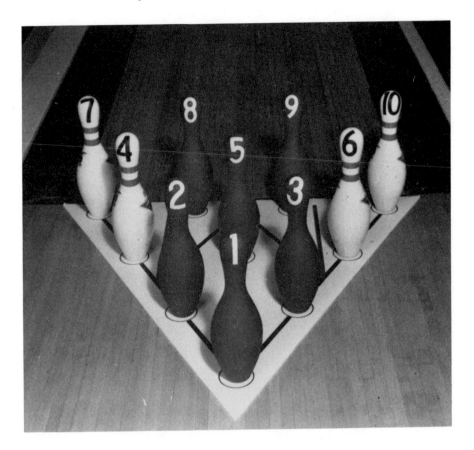

The 4-6-7-10 Impossible Split
Starting Position: Far Right or Far Left

This split results when your ball goes in directly on the nose or headpin without much action. It is a dread split and fortunately occurs infrequently. Take advantage of its scoring possibilities and count as many pins as you can. From your experience, you will know whether you convert the 4-7-10 or the 6-7-10 split more often and so pretend that you have either one of those. Forget about the fourth pin up. By converting the 4-7-10 or 6-7-10 out of this combination, you might get lucky and spill either the 7- or 10-pin forward to make the entire split. If you do, ABC will reward you with a special arm patch, the occurrence is so rare!

The 7–10 Impossible Split
Starting Position: Far Left or Far Right

This is a freak hit, fortunately not seen very frequently. It is a double tap in that both corner pins are left on what appears to be a solid strike hit. In the single tap only the 7-pin or the 10-pin remains standing. When you get this split, practice on your most difficult pin unless you need count. Then, practice on the one you are most certain you can make.

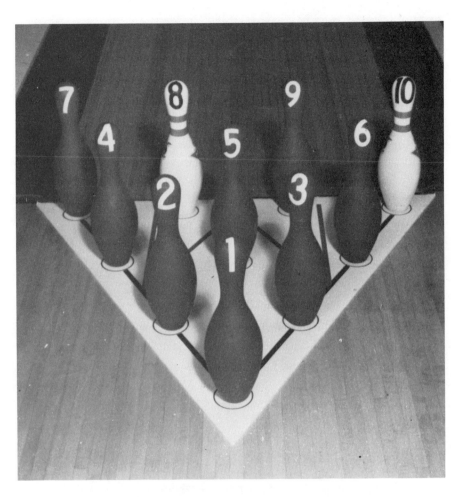

The 8–10 Impossible Split
Starting Position: Strike Position, Brooklyn Line

This split usually occurs when your ball dies or flattens on a pocket 1–3 hit. It is a nasty split and a discouraging one because you came close to a strike. Don't lose the opportunity to practice on the 10-pin—that is, if you are bowling in practice. You might even practice on the 3–10 split by imagining the 3-pin in front of the 10-pin. If you are in competition, count your easiest pin, whichever one it is. Bowl for the 8-pin from Strike Position, Brooklyn Line.

The 7–9 Impossible Split
Starting Position: Far Right or Left Center

This means split pops up on an apparent strike hit and indicates loss of action on the first ball. Use it to your benefit, though, by practicing on your hardest pin. If you have been missing the 7-pin frequently, work on it. Try moving a board or two one way or the other to see what effect the moves have on your ball action. In league play, get your easiest pin and the greatest count possible.

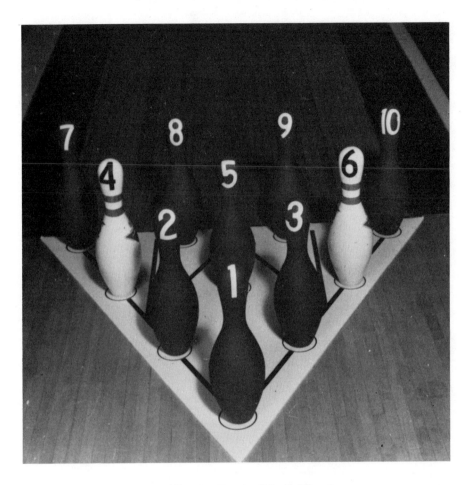

The 4–6 Impossible Split
Starting Position: Far Right or Far Left

This split, like the 4–6–7–10, happens when your ball hits too high on the headpin. In competition, bowl at your easiest pin and be sure to convert it. In practice, bowl at your hardest pin and try to hit the difficult pin in a particular spot: its left side, its right side, or exactly in the middle. Or you might practice on an imaginary 4–7–10 or 6–7–10 split and try to clip the 4- or 6-pin thin enough to slide over and take out the imaginary 7- or 10-pin. If you do it, it is as much fun as making it in an official game.

The 4-6-7-9-10 Impossible Split
Starting Position: Far Left

This is another one of those splits that happens when your ball hits too high on the headpin. It is as frightening as its counterpart, the 4-6-7-10, but oddly it is considerably easier to make even though it is considered one of the impossibles. The trick here is to make the 6-9-10 with a ball that will force the 6-pin to glance off the 9-pin and carom across the lane to help take out the other two pins, the 4- and 7-pins. It is a spectacular conversion and one well worth working on. And even if you don-t get the 4- and 7-pins, you have picked up the maximum in count, anyway!

The 5-7-10 Split

Talk about impossible splits! This is a real beauty. Fortunately, it does not happen very often. It occurs when the headpin is hit right on the nose and not much pin action results. It is believed that this split had been converted only once in the history of bowling. (There may have been other conversions that we don't know about.) Practice your 5-7 or your 5-10, that's all you can do!

7
HOW TO
PRACTICE AT
THE LANES

If you wish to become a good bowler it is necessary that you carry out a regular routine of practice, both on the lanes and away from the lanes in the privacy of your home or office.

First, let us consider the best ways of practicing at the lanes. Using these ideas for a practice routine, I am sure that even the busiest individual will be able to find time to fit in a few times of practice bowling each week.

HOW OFTEN?

Nearly all top professional bowlers practice every day. Some roll only a few games, some as many as a hundred when they feel the need to standardize their deliveries or work out some problem. I know very well that the average bowler cannot bowl as many games as that. The cost in money and in time would be prohibitive. I suggest, however, that the average bowler try to practice at least three lines, or games, of bowling per week and that he carry out this practice with definite objectives in mind.

CHOOSE YOUR PRACTICE TIME CAREFULLY

Here are a few good suggestions on how to practice at the lanes. First, always try to arrange your practice session at a time when the lanes are either dark or on the quiet side. You need to bowl alone in order to get as much peace and quiet as you can get. When the bowling season begins, go to the various lanes in your neighborhood and ask the manager to let you know the schedules of forthcoming leagues. You will always be able to find an interval either before or after a league bowls or an interval between leagues when the lanes will have less play and therefore be quieter for practice.

Ask the manager to put you on a lane away from other bowlers and ask him, also, to keep other bowlers off adjacent lanes as long as possible. Make a friend of the bowling manager. Tell him that you are practicing to improve your bowling; then keep him informed of your progress. Show him your good scores. By making him your friend you will improve your chances of getting "good practice" as contrasted to "bad practice" where you are distracted by other bowlers and confusion around you.

YOUR DELIVERY

Shadow Ball Practice

At first, work on your delivery by rolling what are called *shadow balls*. Ask the lane manager to keep the pins up in the rack of the deck until you tell him to set them. He might even cut his price per bowling game if you shadow bowl because his pins are obviously getting less wear and tear in a shadow game than they would in a real game.

Developing Uniformity

Then, really concentrate on standardizing your delivery. Note where you are placing your target foot (the left if you are right-handed). Choose your spot at the break of the boards and proceed to bowl without any pins. You will find that since there are no pins to be knocked down your entire attention can be focused on any one of the various segments of your successful bowling delivery.

Work on one particular part of your delivery at a time and make notes in your little black book as you go along. Check your hand position at delivery, whether you are consistently releasing the ball with explosive finger action. Check whether the ball is rolling over your target at the splice or not, and whether you are getting the ball well out over the line the 12 to 14 inches that I recommend. Work on your timing. Try to roll the ball at exactly the same speed every time. Work on your routine. Imagine that you are performing on television and the cameras are on you. See yourself going to the rack and picking up your ball. See yourself getting set on the approach, placing your target foot, sighting

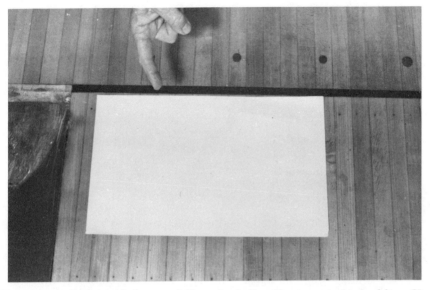

Here's a good idea to help you deliver the ball well out over the foul line. You can use a clean sheet of paper or a white towel. Put it at the foul line and practice lofting your ball over the line so that it doesn't move the paper or towel. You will soon see when you are dropping the ball too close to the foul line and be able to make the necessary correction in your delivery.

your arrow or line target. Picture yourself making a smooth delivery with a good follow-through. Use a watch with a sweep second hand to time yourself from the moment you proceed to the rack until you return to the scorer's table. Try to make this routine exactly the same every time. If you do it will pay off in helping you to standardize your delivery. You want to become a bowling machine capable of rolling a strike on every first ball. A machine performs in regular rhythm. You must do so, too.

Weak Points

Work on the weak points of your game. If you are having trouble making the 7-pin or the 10-pin, shoot at the pesky pin with a shadow

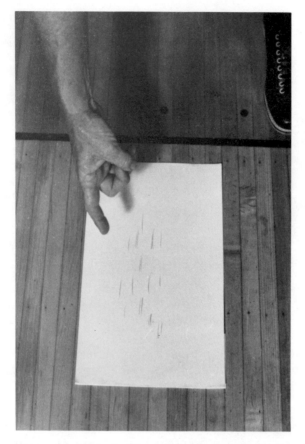

Here's the way to use a sheet of white paper taped onto the lane just over the foul line in order to show you where your ball is touching down on the lane in your delivery. You can check your consistency in direction as well as the amount of loft by the marks on the paper. You should practice until your cluster of marks is consistently in the same place within a fraction of an inch or two everytime you roll the ball.

ball until you can see your ball going through the 7-pin or 10-pin spot every time.

Let us presume that the first part of such practice amounts to two full

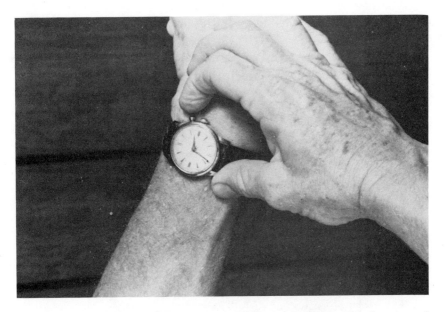

Practice your bowling approach and delivery routine with the use of a stopwatch. Time yourself from the time you take the ball from the return rack until you come back to your seat. Another idea: Have a friend time the speed of your ball down the lane. Try for consistent timing of your routine.

games of bowling. For the latter part of your practice you should ask the manager to set the pins for you.

Making Your Spares

Then work on making your spares. Don't bowl at the setup to make a strike on your first ball. Bowl, for example, at the right hand baby split—the 3–10–on your first ball and watch to see whether you would have made it. You will find that you have a good leave left. The headpin should still be standing and then you can practice your strike ball by rolling for the 1–3 pocket even if the 3-pin has been knocked down on your first practice shot.

Try doing the same thing on the left-hand side by aiming for the 2–7 or even by trying to take out the 7-pin alone. Alternate shots at the 7-pin and the 10-pin.

What you are trying to do is get complete control of your delivery. You will do just that if you practice in this intelligent manner.

Dawson Taylor is demonstrating the use of white adhesive tape on the lane from the foul line to the target area. He has also placed two paper cups at the break of the boards to narrow his target and to tell him when he misses his target on one side or the other. The paper cups should be placed so that there is increasingly less target area until the bowler can hit the precise line he wants.

HOW TO INCREASE YOUR PRACTICE TIME

Roll as many practice games as you can fit into your weekly schedule. Do not practice when you are overly tired or when you "don't feel like practicing." Always stop when you begin to tire. Be very careful not to hurt your fingers by bowling too much at one time. If your thumb or finger starts to burn, stop at once or you may work up a blister that will prevent you from bowling comfortably for a long time. Incidentally, that is another reason why I recommend that you wear a bowling glove which will take much of the wear of the delivery rather than your tender skin.

One of my pupils was a businessman who was averaging 165 in two club leagues. He came to me and asked me how he could improve his game by 20 pins or more. I told him about shadow bowling and gave him some of the other suggestions I have given you.

Here is the schedule of practice he worked out, one that did not interfere with his carrying on a normal, successful business life.

He bowled in two different late afternoon leagues. They started at 5:30 P.M. He arranged to get to the lanes by 5:00 P.M. and was able to practice one to one and a half games before the league started. On Saturday afternoons he would go to a neighborhood lane and bowl three or four games with his son. Sometimes on Sunday mornings he would bowl with his wife and once more he could roll three or four games to add to his practice total. During his business week he made it his custom to go to a different lane at noon. He would get a quick sandwich at the lunch counter and squeeze in three more games of practice before he went back to his office. So you see he was able to get in about 19 or 20 practice games per week. Inside of one year that bowler had improved his average to the 180 range. Then he tapered off his practice routine. He had achieved the goal he had set for himself, and at the 180 mark he became champion of both of his club leagues.

So you see what can be done with intelligent practice. I recommend it highly to you if you wish to become a better bowler!

VARY PRACTICE CONDITIONS

If you can arrange to do so, make an effort to bowl under as many different lane conditions as possible. Some lanes are known as *pie alleys,* easy to score on, others as *brickyards,* tough to score on. In some houses a certain pair of lanes may become well-known as an especially high-scoring pair. I remember well one pair at Crest Lanes in Detroit, Michigan, lane numbers 11 and 12, which were famous for producing high scores. One unusual record was set there a number of years ago when Reno Ministrelli of the Falcon Wine Team and George Young, captain of the famous Pfeiffer Brewing team rolled back-to-back (or side-to-side?) 300 games during a team match. Each was bowling in the number three slot on his team and the bowlers kept matching each other's strikes one after the other until the tenth frame. First Reno stepped up in the tenth frame and rammed his three strikes home. The crowd went wild, of course, as George waited patiently for his turn to roll his tenth frame. George's three strikes were equally as solid and the record of two simultaneous 300s went into the books. I wonder how much credit should have been given to the soft lane beds of number 11 and number 12 lanes?

When you are in a bowling slump it helps to get your confidence back by bowling on easy-scoring lanes. So when your game goes sour, as it does sometimes for everyone, search out a high-scoring pair of lanes for practice and get your confidence back.

The same thing holds true in reverse. If you are able to score well on tough lanes or under unusually difficult lane conditions you can score even better on normal lanes. Look for low-scoring lanes, too, and by practicing on them you can make yourself unafraid of any lane. Your friendly lane manager can tell you when he has freshly oiled the lanes so that you can practice bowling on slippery lanes. He will tell you, too, when he has put up new pins with solid straight-edged bottoms that will give you your money's worth as you bowl. You should try to bowl against three-pound-six-ounce pins as often as you can. When you can strike against heavy wood your confidence will rise and you will never be afraid of bowling against such pins in a tournament. It follows, too, that you will be even more confident against the lighter wood.

I knew a Midwest bowler, Don Wilson, who arranged to buy his own sets of pins from the Northern Maple Company in Upper Michigan. He donated them to the bowling lane where he customarily practiced. When he would practice, the lane manager (undoubtedly a most understanding man) would yell down to his pit crew to "set those logs for Mr. Wilson." Mr. Wilson was a 170 average bowler at the time. The sound of the bowling ball hitting against four-pound wood is simply awesome, he told me. Against such wood you get only the pins you deserve. A year later Mr. Wilson was averaging over 180 and eventually got into the 190s. He was another example of sensible practice that paid off.

WARM-UP GAMES

Many bowlers need a game or more to warm up before a bowling session. Sometimes it is difficult to arrange to do this. One league follows another in rapid succession and most of the time the league bowler has time for no more than a few practice rolls before the lights go on.

There are many ways to get in some practice ahead of time. If you cannot get out onto the lanes themselves, you can and should warm up physically in the locker room by performing as many as possible of the bowling exercises we discuss in Chapter 9. One suggestion I have for you is that you actually toss the ball back and forth with the help of a fellow bowler. I do not recommend this practice for the woman bowler but definitely suggest it for the male bowler who has at least moderate strength. Once you get the trick of catching the ball in mid-air the exercise becomes mutually profitable. Each bowler should take turns tossing the ball to the other at about a five- to six-foot distance. Obviously, the ball should be tossed easily. Each bowler should concentrate on his finger release, feeling the thumb release and the ball come off his fingers with spin.

Fred Wolf, the famous bowling commentator of early television shows, was a fine bowler himself and told this story on himself. He had an absolute phobia about bowling in a tournament without practicing ahead of time. He was bowling in the famous Inter-Club Tournament at Buffalo. Cleveland Athletic Club, Detroit Athletic Club, Buffalo Athletic Club, and the Pittsburgh Athletic Association each fielded teams of 10 bowlers in round robin matches over two days.

Fred was scheduled to bowl in the 10:00 A.M. doubles competition. He would get two shadow balls and no more than that before he began to bowl on his shift. Fred knew this, so the night before he bowled he made inquiries about public lanes nearby. He located one a half-mile away and made arrangements for it to be opened at 8:30 A.M. so that he could practice. At 8:25 A.M. of the tournament day, a taxi took Fred to the lane. He rolled two games as the taxi driver waited outside. Then Fred came back to the Buffalo Athletic Club nicely warmed up.

Whether it was coincidence or not, Fred rolled strikes the first eight frames in a row in his opening game. He drew the 5–7 split in his ninth frame, converted it, and went out in 278. He and his partner won the doubles that day. Fred's preparation and practice paid off. His body was ready and mentally he had convinced himself that with adequate practice he would perform well and he did.

CONCENTRATE

When you practice at the lanes, bowl seriously. By that I mean, do not roll any careless shots. Imagine that every roll of the ball is for an ABC championship and has to be a good one. Use the same routine on every practice roll that you would use in actual play.

It is said that Ben Hogan, the great golfer and famous practicer, never changed his routine while practicing. He would step away from the ball on every shot, step back, sight his target, go through his waggles, concentrate, and then make his stroke. I want you to do the same thing in bowling. Never roll a careless shot. If you establish this attitude in your practice, I guarantee that your average will climb to your own personal peak!

8
HOW TO
PRACTICE AT HOME
OR AT THE OFFICE

Here is a picture of Brenda working on her delivery at home. She has put down a yardstick on the floor of her recreation room and keeps walking her four step delivery over and over. After many hours of such practice, the line of the yardstick becomes so indelibly impressed on the bowler's mind that he continues to see it in his mind's eye when he bowls on the lanes.

It is very important that you learn to practice certain elements of your bowling delivery at home in your recreation room, or for that matter in any room which has a vinyl tile covering that can become a mock bowling lane practice approach.

Get some one-inch-wide adhesive tape and put it down on the floor with a *T* upside down to indicate your starting position. If you can stretch this line out to 16 or even 18 feet, the effect is even better. Here's how to use the white line: Put your target foot on the left side of the line. Standing as if you are going to deliver a ball down that line and without looking down at your feet, push out an imaginary ball and step forward at exactly the same time with your right foot. Then look down and see where your right foot has taken you. Mark that spot on the tape with a pencil.

By constantly rehearsing that first step and making sure that you are stepping exactly the same distance each first step, you will begin to standardize your footwork. Repeat it over and over again.

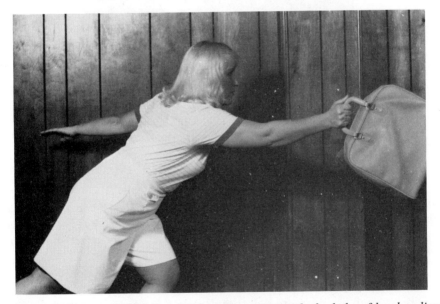

Here is Brenda practicing her full bowling swing with the help of her bowling bag. At first she worked with the empty bag, then added other items such as her shoes and her repair kit, and finally put her bowling ball inside to give her a full swing approximating that of the bowling ball on the lane. This is an excellent practice to help develop rhythm and timing of the delivery.

Here is a picture of Brenda practicing her follow-through and her squeeze finger action at the line. Notice how she has her eyes riveted on a spot down the lane in front of her. It helps sometimes to place some object out at the imaginary break of the boards.

Then, having perfected your first step distance, you may start to use an object such as an iron in your bowling hand to represent the bowling ball. Lengthen your steps into a full delivery, paying particular attention to bending your left knee as you slide. Since the iron has a nice handle on it (unlike a bowling ball) there is no danger that you will let it go as you follow through in your mock delivery.

I have also suggested that you consider using a metronome to improve your rhythm. You can count to yourself, too, in regular cadence but when you make that final move to deliver the imaginary ball over the line I want you to do it with increasing force — with zip and with authority.

You will find that by practicing your delivery down the white line your mind will be indelibly impressed with the line. When you bowl in actual play on the lanes you will continue to see it and follow its perfect direction down the lane.

You can practice the squeeze technique, too, in the privacy of your recreation room or office. At least once every day, take your bowling ball and put it on the floor before you. Do the squeeze 15 to 20 times in a row. Try to perform the action the same way every time, with your third and fourth fingers under the ball in your usual delivery position. You may also benefit by using a rubber ball soft enough to be compressed to the same degree that your fingers need to be compressed in an actual squeeze of the ball. Watch the movement of your thumb as it comes forward. Then when you bowl you can visualize your finger action more easily as you release the ball with squeeze action. From the beginning of this squeeze practice, keep track of the number of revolutions you can impart to the ball with the squeeze technique. You will be surprised to see how quickly you gain not only finger strength, but also increased awareness of the feeling you must have in your fingers, hand, and wrist to produce the most powerful bowling action at delivery.

Another pleasant factor about practice at home or at the office is that the price is right — you can bowl 15 games in your imagination without it costing you a cent.

9
THE
EXERCISE
PROGRAM

In order to become a champion bowler it is obvious that you must put your bowling machine, your body, into the best possible physical condition to accomplish your goal.

You do not want to be carrying around 10 or more extra pounds on your frame. If you are overweight it follows with great certainty that you will find yourself tiring on the last game of a series and unable to roll the ball with your usual speed. So if you happen to be overweight, the first thing I suggest is that you take a good look at yourself in the mirror. Decide that those extra pounds have to go. Start a reasonable slimming diet—no crashes because they simply don't work!—and slowly but surely take off the pounds until you are satisfied that you have reached your own personal goal in weight reduction. Be sure to consult your family physician before you diet so that he can check your blood pressure and perhaps suggest some vitamins as a diet supplement.

Try to live what I call "the moderate life." Eat carefully, drink carefully or not at all, get proper rest at regular hours, and exercise in moderation.

Exercises that strengthen a bowler's legs are the most important he can do. Your sliding leg takes a great deal of punishment as it brings your body to a halt at the foul line. Many times I have encountered a sticky approach which caused my sliding foot to stop prematurely and jolt my entire body. So concentrate on exercises that strengthen your legs.

I recommend that you begin a walking program at once. Every day you should walk at least a mile at a moderately rapid pace. Then lengthen your walk to two miles a day, perhaps with one mile in the morning and one in the evening. It does not matter whether you do your mileage all at once; just do it, faithfully, rain or shine.

If jogging is attractive to you, then by all means jog your way to leg strength and an increase in your stamina. I myself am a jogger and try to get in from two to four miles every day. I like bicycle riding also, and find that it is very helpful in strengthening my legs and keeping them in top condition.

Brenda shows us a leg-strengthening exercise here. She leans against a wall with her hands out in front of her and gradually moves her body back farther and farther from the wall. The hamstrings are stretched in this way. Bowlers are often subject to leg cramps. If this exercise is carried out faithfully, you will never have a leg cramp.

If you carry out a regular program of walking, bicycling, or jogging you will find that your physical condition will improve and soon you will reach a better condition than you have ever enjoyed. Not only will your "bowling machine" improve—your whole life will be richer with a new glow of health.

I would like to recommend that you get a modest set of weights. Get some barbells that weigh no more than 15 to 20 pounds. I believe that since the bowling ball weighs 16 pounds, the average bowler as well as the professional bowler should constantly work with weights that duplicate the weight and strain encountered while bowling.

Part of your exercise routine should include swinging the barbell back and forth in a mock bowling delivery. It is useful to do this exercise in front of a full-length mirror. Check to see that your body is square to the mirror and that you are taking the barbell straight back and straight through. Be careful to hang onto the weight or you may lose the mirror! I once knew a bowler who used to practice a mock delivery in his basement before a big mirror. He would swing his bowling ball and hang onto it as he made his mock delivery. One day he failed to hang onto the ball. He said you never saw so much broken glass in your life!

Part of your daily exercise routine should be devoted to stretching exercises. In order to bowl well you need to have a supple body and well-toned muscles. A well-stretched muscle also is less likely to become tense under pressure. I suggest that you buy any one of the many excellent books on the market today which show pictures of exercises. I find it easier to follow the instructions of such a book than it is to read text and try to follow it. One book that I have found most rewarding is *The Complete Guide to Total Fitness* by Jan Percival, Lloyd Percival, and Joe Taylor. This book is especially good in its recommendations for hand and arm exercises. Here are a few exercises that are especially good for bowlers:

1. The Resistance Press Down

Extend both your arms. Make a fist with your right hand and place your left palm over it. Press down with your upper hand, resisting with your fist. Hold for six seconds, relax, and then switch hands. Repeat from 6 to 12 times each arm and rest.

2. Single Arm Resistance

Extend your right arm down in front of your body. Bend your left arm and grasp your right wrist. Flex your right arm, bringing your wrist upward toward your left shoulder. The left arm resists the right all

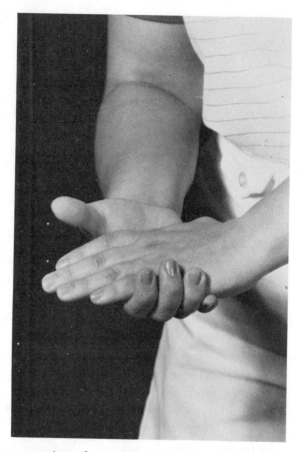

Brenda is demonstrating a form of Hand Press here. She has her bowling hand at her right side and is pressing down on the open palm with her left hand at maximum pressure. You must be careful not to strain the wrist with this exercise, however. Experiment and find the best hand placement and pressure for you.

through this upward move. Change hands. Repeat from 4 to 8 times each arm and rest.

Isometric exercise is exercise in which there is no movement. The basic objective is to meet the immovable object with irresistible force. The theory of isometrics was first popularized in the 1950s by German

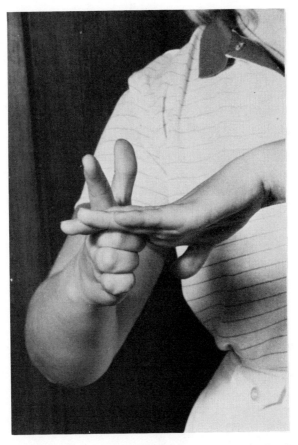

This isometric exercise is especially aimed at strengthening the third and fourth fingers of the bowler's hand. By exerting strong downward pressure by the left hand while pulling up on the third and fourth fingers of the right hand, the fingers and wrist of the bowling hand are strengthened and better able to resist the weight of the ball in the backswing.

researchers, Hethinger and Muller. The idea is that tension of a muscle held at 66 percent of maximum for six seconds at a time would build strength.

I use many isometric exercises myself and recommend that you try a few, too. Your hand, your fingers, and your wrist need to be very strong

Brenda demonstrates the isometric exercise to strengthen the bowler's wrist. By pressing down on the clenched right fist and holding for six seconds with the left hand, Brenda will strengthen her right wrist immeasurably after a month or more of regular exercise. I recommend this exercise to you. It is easy to do with very effective results.

to resist the weight of the heavy bowling ball. While we are allowed to use wrist protectors to help keep the wrist from breakdown in the backswing or at the delivery, by using isometric exercises that focus on finger, wrist, and hand strength the bowler may be able to strengthen his bowling arm to the point that he no longer needs a wrist protector.

Here are some isometric exercises for hand, wrist, and arm strength:

1. The Hooked Finger Pull

Hook your fingers together in front of your chest with your arms a little lower than chest height. Pull outward with a steady pull for six seconds. Repeat up to 10 times and rest.

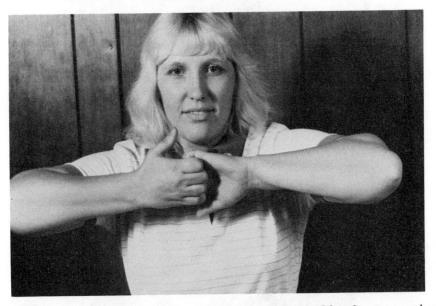

Brenda is doing the Hooked Finger Pull. She has hooked her fingers together in front of her chest with her arms a little lower than chest height. By pulling outward with a steady pull the fingers of the bowling hand will be strengthened. This is also a rehearsal for the feeling that the fingers must have when they release the bowling ball with the squeeze action.

2. The Desk Lift or Table Lift

Put your bowling hand in the squeeze position with your third finger curved under the top of your desk or a heavy table. Lift straight up, applying resistance to your third and fourth fingers. Hold the resistance for six seconds at a time. Repeat 10 times and rest.

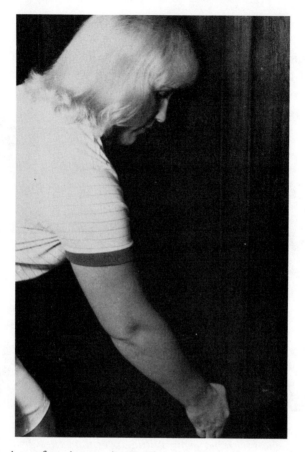

Here Brenda is performing an isometric exercise against a wall in order to strengthen her fingers, her wrist, and all the muscles of her forearm. By lifting straight ahead in this exercise it is possible to impress on the mind the necessity for lifting straight out over the lanes in a real delivery.

A good way to count the seconds is to say to yourself, "one thousand and one, one thousand and two," and so on.

If you carry out a sensible exercise program aimed particularly at strengthening the muscles used in bowling, not only will your bowling improve but your whole attitude toward life will get a tremendous lift. Such a program has worked for me. I know it will for you too!

10
THE MENTAL
SIDE OF
BOWLING

BUILDING CONFIDENCE

The dictionary tells us that confidence is characterized by a "strong, reliant, and bold belief in oneself; by freedom from fear, doubt, and worry. It may imply a firm feeling of success. " Without intending to be boastful, I would like to say that I am a confident bowler. But I have not always been a confident bowler. I was a beginner bowler just like you a little over 25 years ago. The 7-pin was my nemesis; I could never make it with my wide-breaking left-hand hook.

I realized early that there were many holes in my bowling game. I needed to develop a repeating, consistent strike ball and I needed to learn to convert every possible spare I might leave. I had to learn, too, when to try to make a split and when not to—when to go for the count.

By assiduous practice on literally thousands of bowling lanes, slowly I built my game on a sound foundation of good rhythm, consistent speed, accuracy of aim, and ability to hit my target spot. And most important of all, I learned to consistently produce the strong finger and wrist action at the line that imparts dynamic action to the ball as it leaves the hand on the way to the headpin.

As I achieved each one of my goals I could sense that I had stepped to a higher level of success in my bowling career. When I finally conquered the problem of the 7-pin and could count on making 9 out of every 10 2–7 baby splits, when I could fit my ball every time between the 5–6 and slide the 5-pin over into the 10-pin time after time when I drew the 5–10, at last I knew that I had the spare side of my game under control. I had reached a wonderful plateau in my bowling, because simultaneously (probably as a result of the many hours I worked on the spares), my strike ball had come along well, too. I finally broke through to win my first professional bowling tournament. That check—only $500.00 compared to prizes of $40,000 or $50,000 in tourneys today—looked like a million dollars to me.

I tried to make myself a good bowler, and I was able to do so. You, too, can achieve nearly any level of bowling prowess you wish provided that you devote a great deal of attention and time to doing it. It will also help if your physical body is built for the sport, if you have a natural sense of timing, and most of all, if you desire to excel.

I firmly believe that the winners are separated from the losers mainly by that desire to excel—that drive that keeps the athlete coming back again and again after a disappointing performance in sport.

I promise you that if you will take my advice to heart, study the mathematics of all the spares and splits as I point them out to you in this book, and set aside a reasonable amount of time for intelligent practice at and away from the lanes, you will inevitably become a good bowler. You may even become a champion bowler, holding a 200 average for an entire season—or, failing that great goal, become a competent bowler among your peers, capable of matching them strike for strike and having a wonderful time doing it for the rest of your life.

Confidence in bowling is built upon the memory of repeated success. You will have repeated success in making your spares, splits, and strikes if you follow my method of instruction. And you will become a confident bowler!

KEEP YOUR COOL

Have you ever wondered why some bowlers are winners and others are not? I'm sure you have seen a bowler without the bowling form you would expect in someone who "gets the pins," and yet he does get them much of the time. That bowler has the ability to concentrate. You will notice, too, that he delivers the ball with authority, with a snap or drive at the last second that seems to tell the ball, "now go and get those pins!" Furthermore, you will seldom see that bowler let anger take away his concentration.

How often we see bowlers get angry when they leave a 10-pin or draw a split they think they did not deserve. Every bowler must realize that bowling is not an exact science, and that a good percentage of his strikes and spares are due to plain luck—the lucky bounce or spin of a pin that takes down a pin he should have missed. So knowing that luck plays a great factor in good bowling, the "lucky" bowler takes advantage of luck by delivering his ball with good speed, with authority, and with confidence that he has rolled the best ball he possibly could. When that stubborn 10-pin stands he does not allow himself to get upset, but accepts his fate and carefully controls his emotions so his spare shot can be made with calm mind and body.

In my years of tournament bowling I watched many bowlers go through unbelievable body gyrations after delivering the ball over the line. I have watched them jump into the air on a strike, and fall face downward on the lane in despair when the pins do not go down the way the bowler thinks they should. In my attempt to become not only a good bowler but a champion bowler, I decided that such antics were not for me. I felt that if I did not keep my emotions under strict control, I might be rolling the ball with my adrenaline high and could roll it at a greater speed than I wanted. More and more I became convinced that absolute control of speed was essential to my bowling game. If I could roll any ball with accuracy and control my speed as well, I could hit the pocket every time. Of course, I didn't score a strike every time, but I did find that with more attention paid to hitting my target, and with consistent speed of the ball I was able to bowl a greater proportion of strikes than I ever had before.

I was determined to control my emotions, and I'm pleased to say that after years of concentration I have achieved an evenness of temper which I'm sure has contributed greatly to my success.

A year or so ago I noticed a new "hot" bowler on the bowling tour. When he rolled a strike he would jump all over the lanes, gyrate and make gestures with his fist, and grimace with a snarling face as if to say, "Take that strike and that strike!" And yet today, that bowler—as well as other bowlers who conduct themselves in the same manner—is seldom heard from in tournaments. Is there a lesson there? I think so, and I pass it on to you. Control your emotions when you bowl. Don't get too excited or too depressed at what happens on the lane. Bowl your best at all times, but don't take it so seriously you don't get any fun out of this wonderful game.

PRACTICE THE POSITIVE

In this book I am sure you have noticed that I put a great deal of emphasis on practice. I firmly believe that you should not only practice the physical side of bowling but practice the mental side of bowling, too. You should accustom yourself to bowling under game conditions—that is, "under pressure"—so that when a pressure situation arises in competition you will be so accustomed to the feeling you can say to yourself, "This is nothing more than what I was doing successfully every time last week in practice."

There is a trick known to psychologists as "the transfer of identical elements." An example of the use of this idea is when basketball coaches set the game clock at "three minutes to go" and make their players practice free throws in situations which closely approximate late-game conditions. Sinking foul shots under pressure conditions is what wins most games—not practicing making them when you are relaxed and physically fresh.

So that is why I recommend intensive practice under game conditions for the bowler who wishes to succeed in bowling.

Let us say that the 5–7 split is one of your most difficult conversions. I believe that the ordinary bowler who can average 170 pins or more in a season should be able to correct the 5–7 one out of every two times. The practice routine for the good bowler on the 5–7 (or any other makeable split) should be carried out in this way: Begin a study of your present success in converting the split. Keep track of how many out of ten you make when you begin your intensive campaign to increase your conversion average. At first, you might make one conversion out of ten. But by using the Strike Position, 5–7 Line; checking your target foot at the start; sliding straight; and watching to see that your ball is rolling over your target spot you will inevitably begin to convert the 5–7 more frequently than you have before.

I want you to brain-wash yourself as you do this practice. Say to yourself, "I'm not bowling for the 5–7. I don't care if I make it. All I'm doing is rolling my normal strike ball from a slightly inside position. I know that if I roll it normally I'll make the 5–7 because the ball will be coming in thin on the 5-pin." The mind can think of only one thought at a time. Since that is true, the trick is to make your mind think the positive thought, "I will roll my normal strike ball," rather than the negative one, "I have to make this horrible split."

Keep track of your conversions and your misses. For a while you may see no improvement, and then suddenly you will find yourself relaxing and not caring whether you make the split or not. Then you will be making the split more frequently. You may even get up to a 50–50 rate. What you have done is banish the negative thought, "I must make the 5–7 split or lose a lot of pins" and replace it with the positive thought, "I'm going to roll my normal strike ball. I don't care what happens down there at the end of the lane. The fact that I have the 5–7 is immaterial to me."

I promise you the results will be a surprise to you. You will succeed in making that split or any other split more frequently than you ever have in the past.

11
THE PHYSIOLOGY, PHYSICS, AND MATHEMATICS OF BOWLING

PHYSIOLOGY OF BOWLING: TENSED OUTER MUSCLE THEORY

I would like to call your attention to what I call the "Tensed Outer Muscle Theory of Bowling." It is very important that you understand it because when you do, you will be more aware of the state of your own arm tension when you bowl. You will understand what tension should be present, and what tension should not be present.

Briefly, the theory means that when the outside muscles of the arm and fingers are in tension (and therefore in control of the bowling delivery) there will be a lessened tendency toward the wrist-turning or finger rotation which cause a wrongly thrown ball by *topping* or *overturning* — there will be only the proper lift forward, giving the ball the correct start after the squeeze of the fingers.

Throughout the pendulum action of the bowling arc backward and forward through the moment of delivery, the outer muscles of the arm and hand remain tense and are kept under constant tension. The elbow, acting as a hinge, breaks directly upward in a plane perpendicular to the floor at the moment of delivery. From start to finish, the entire shoulder and arm proceed backward and forward without any rotation clockwise or counterclockwise away from the beginning hand and arm position.

I'd like you to prove something to yourself. Reach out in front of your body with your right hand and feel the tension in the outer muscles of your arm. Technically, these are known as the extensors. Now, with your arm extended, close your fist tightly and you will feel the inner muscles of your arm become activated. These are the flexors. Then open your fist so that only the last three fingers are clenched. You will find that your thumb and first finger are controlled by different flexor muscles than the other three; and you have proof that the thumb and forefinger can be relaxed and yet allow you the clenched action of the squeeze delivery.

Here is another interesting experiment for you to carry out in the physiology of bowling. Clasp your left hand tightly just above your right wrist. Attempt to turn your right wrist counterclockwise by using the right wrist alone. You cannot do it! Your ability to turn the wrist—

and consequently the fingers, too—arises in a turning movement which begins in the elbow socket. The rest arises in the shoulder and is accomplished by the elbow leaving the side of the body. All of this gives strong physiological basis for the conclusion that "the elbow, acting as a hinge, must break directly upward in a plane perpendicular to the floor," and also further substantiates the necessity for *squareness to the line*, or keeping the elbow tight to the right side and not allowing it to stray out from the body and thus permit unwanted wrist or finger rotation at the moment of delivery.

PHYSICAL PROOF OF THE NEED TO LEAN FORWARD AS YOU RELEASE THE BALL

Here's another physical exercise I want you to try: Stand up perfectly straight as if you are facing an imaginary foul line. Now draw your right arm back in an imaginary swing. Notice that when your arm reaches a 40- to 45-degree angle you begin to feel a distinct binding sensation in your shoulder muscles and are somewhat prevented from making any worthy backswing.

Now, with your arm still extended at the 40- to 45-degree angle behind you, lean forward from the waist and feel the freedom that immediately occurs. Your shoulder muscles no longer bind. Now you can complete a backswing to shoulder height without difficulty. The obvious conclusion of this physical experiment is that you must lean forward while making your approach to the line and explosion point. If you do not, you cannot accomplish a satisfactory backswing.

PHYSICS AND DYNAMICS OF THE BOWLING BALL WITH EXPLOSIVE FINGER ACTION

Throughout the armswing—forward, back, and starting downward—the weight of the ball remains primarily on the bowler's thumb (this presumes that the bowler's grip is a correct one). When the ball reaches the bottom of the swing and as the bowler begins to move it

When I stand up straight and push my arm into an imaginary backswing, I can feel the tension start in my upper chest when my arm reaches about a 45-degree angle. If I allowed my backswing to stop at this point it is evident that it would be a restricted one without much power.

forward and out over the foul line, the weight of the ball is transferred from the thumb to the fingers. In fact, just before the full release of the ball the ball is balanced in a precarious position on the fingers alone. That is one of the reasons why the fingers must be held in tension, and not be slack or relaxed until that last split second when they can import

Now I lean forward and perform the same imaginary backswing. See how much freer my backswing is. I can reach parallel before there is any constriction of the muscles in my upper body. I believe that if you will perform these same physical actions you will come to understand the importance of leaning forward in your delivery as you make your backswing.

the explosive finger action to the ball.

During this last fraction of a second the action of the fingers will either make or break your ball. I would like you to try this little exercise to dramatize the finger action at delivery. Have a friend stand in front of you as you grip your bowling ball in your normal grip. Hold the ball at chest height and ask him to take the ball away from your hand by pulling it from you. Try to hold onto the ball as long as you can. You will see that the first thing that happens during this maneuver is that your thumb leaves the ball and only the fingers remain on it. The thumb is shorter than the other fingers and therefore it comes out first. Now you can understand why your ball must be lifted, even lofted out onto the lane at delivery. That stretching movement, the reaching of your hand and arm forward, allows your thumb to get out of the ball (which it must do) and allows the fingers to do their work.

Picture a clock face drawn on your ball. Your thumb is the pin that holds the hands of the clock in place. Your thumb should always be pointing toward the center of the ball. When you reach the foul line this means that your thumb is pointing straight at the floor when the ball is at the bottom of your pendulum swing.

At the instant of release your thumb should be pointing down the lane straight toward your target. This is the proper thumb position no matter whether you roll a hook, a curve, or a straight ball. If your thumb is not in this position (pointing down the lane) the ball will not be able to leave your hand smoothly and naturally.

To roll what is called a *natural hook* the fingers must remain toward the right back side of the ball throughout the release. If they remain in the 11 o'clock to 5 o'clock position we discussed earlier, the fingers will be able to close on the ball in the finger-snapping motion (or squeeze motion) and lift the ball so that it begins to release from the right or center, toward left or center forward.

Since your ball begins to revolve toward the left you might expect it to run toward the left channel at once. It would do so except that there is a much stronger force operating on the ball once it has been released from the hand. That force is called *forward thrust* or *momentum*.

As your ball rolls down the lane, these two basic forces are operating on it and will control its final action as the ball nears the pins. During the first few feet of travel down the lane the ball is governed completely by its initial forward thrust. While the ball is revolving toward the left, the body of the ball goes straight down the lane (or if not straight down, in the direction it has been rolled) and gradually the strength of the forward thrust decreases. At a certain point, depending upon initial speed, the second force—called *kinetic energy; motion caused by motion*—overcomes the first force and takes control of the ball and causes the ball to hook to the left.

While the ball was sliding and rolling down the lane under the influence of its initial momentum or forward thrust, it continued to revolve on its own axis from right to left or center. Then the friction between the ball and the surface of the lane began to decrease its forward momentum, and the surface of the ball began to grip the surface of the lane and move in the direction of its kinetic energy. The ball, now under the influence of its kinetic energy and revolving toward the left, begins to move left and if properly aimed will hook into the 1–3 pocket.

Note that while I describe a bowling ball delivery which rolls on an 11 o'clock to 5 o'clock axis, I do not mean to preclude a roll which might be from 10 o'clock to 4 o'clock, or even one approaching a 9 o'clock–3 o'clock axis.

These rotations in the orientation of angle of rotation depend upon the hand position in the ball at the last second of release. We will discuss this further when we talk of bowlers who roll the *full roller* bowling ball in contrast to those who *crank* the ball at delivery.

The bowling ball that reaches the 1–3 pocket has considerable kinetic energy left in it. Some of it has been lost in friction while the ball traveled down the lane, and some of it is lost in the spinning of the ball that occurs while it is traveling to the pocket. But granted that enough kinetic energy is left on the ball to do its work, the ball strikes the 1–3 pocket and transfers that kinetic energy to the pins. The pins themselves accept the energy and start to move to the side and against each other, in turn imparting energy to the other pins. The result: a strike, or if there is a freak hit on the pins, a spare or split may result.

Actually, the ball strikes only four pins on the way to causing the ten pins to fall down for a strike. Normally the right-handed bowler's strike

Why It Is So Easy to Miss the 10-Pin

Notice that because the 10-pin is only 2½ inches from the right-hand gutter, you do not get the advantage of the entire ball width on the right side. The same thing holds true, in reverse, for the 7-pin on its left side. Since your target is some seven inches narrower than on other one-pin spares, be especially careful and take advantage of the angle and get the 10-pin or the 7-pin on its "good" side.

ball hits the 1-pin first, then the 2-pin, then the 5-pin, and finally the 9-pin. It then goes into the pit. The bowler must count on the kinetic energy of extra pin action in order to down all ten pins for a strike.

There are two important lessons to be learned from this discussion of the two kinds of energy in a bowling strike. One, it is necessary to roll the ball with *good speed*. By this I mean from moderate speed to slightly more than moderate speed. (We talked about speed in Chapter 3, remember.) The second lesson is the understanding that the fingers

Why It Is So Easy to Miss a Sleeper Pin

It is 22½ inches from the headpin to the 5-pin and also from the 3-pin back to the 9-pin or from the 2-pin to the 8-pin. The other pins such as the 3, 5, and 6 are only one foot apart, so when you study the illustration, you can understand why it is easy for the ball to be deflected off the front pin and miss the rear pin. Tandems such as the 3-9 combination or the 2-8 are tough to convert. Practice hitting them head-on with power to carry through the long distance to the back pin.

must impart the explosive action to the ball as they deliver it out over the foul line, putting enough revolutions on the ball so that they are still causing the ball to rotate left as it strikes the pins. Here's a well-known bowling adage: "The more revolutions the bowler can impart to the ball, the stronger the strike ball"—and usually the better the bowler.

It is surprising how many bowlers miss single-pin spares. When you consider the situation carefully it is hard to believe that any bowler can miss a target nearly 22 inches wide. The ball itself is 8.59 inches in diameter, the pin is 4.76 inches, and you can hit the pin on either side. So you have the pin width and two ball diameters as your target. You should never *miss a one-pin spare!*

Why It Is So Easy to Be Tapped on a 10-Pin, a 7-Pin, or a 4-Pin

Sometimes your strike ball appears to go right under all the pins and starts them revolving in a horizontal plane so that all the pins go down. And then again, sometimes your ball seems to knock the pins straight across the lane. Always remember that you may have a pleasant 15-inch-wide track clearing out pins for you if your pins fly crossways, but if they go straight through you have only a 4-inch track. That's why you will often lose a pin or two on what seems to be a good hit. Don't worry about it; the luck evens out.

12
COMMON FAULTS
AND WHAT TO DO
ABOUT THEM

SIDE-WHEELING

One of the most frequent serious faults which the bowler must avoid is *side-wheeling,* and just as the name implies, it is caused by the bowler turning to the side in clockwise fashion as he starts the ball into its backswing. This results in the bowler taking his body away from the necessary squareness to the line. By turning clockwise the ball is caused to come around the bowler's body; and at the moment of delivery it is rolled with the elbow out, away from the bowler's side, causing an over-turning action, the fingers being on top of the ball and physically in no position to put the necessary finger action on the ball. The ball comes off the thumb and has no action on the pins. Usually this type of delivery will cause a sore thumb as all the weight of the ball is thrown against the thumb instead of being carried in the fingers. The spin of the ball off the thumb causes severe wear on the skin of the thumb.

Cure for the fault of side-wheeling: Keep the body square to the line all the way through the delivery, with the arm close to the body.

BACKSWING WITH AN OUTSIDE ARC

Another major fault the bowler must avoid is the opposite of side-wheeling, and that is taking the ball back in an outside arc, instead of straight back. The result is that the elbow strays from its proper position tight to the bowler's side and in the downswing the ball is caused to roll on a line which crosses inward to the left of the headpin.

Although it is possible for the bowler to impart action to the ball, usually a bad hit results on the left hand side of the headpin — or worse, misses the headpin entirely to the left. Many splits result from such a hit, as we have already seen. Quite often, too, this type of hit results in a topped action at the delivery point, with the fingers ahead of their proper position and consequently in no position to work properly in importing their lifting action at the line. Most important is the fact that with this fault the bowler cannot roll down his intended line.

Here is a view taken from the rear, showing the fault of side-wheeling. It is one of the most serious faults that a bowler can get into as it prevents him from delivering the ball down the line he wants. The body has been turned away from squareness to the foul line and rarely can the bowler recover in time to release the ball properly. The solution is to use an arm-swing that is straight back and straight through and to keep the body square at all times.

This fault is the opposite of side-wheeling. It is caused by the bowler taking the ball in the backswing in a definite outside arc. The result is that the elbow strays from its proper position tight to the bowler's side and the ball rolls on a line crossing inward to the left of the headpin.

Here is the fault of topping the ball *at the foul line. As you can see from the picture I have not followed through with the shot but have stopped short and spun the ball off my thumb. There has been no finger lift, and the result is a ball with no action and one that is often misdirected as well. You should concentrate on keeping the fingers behind the thumb until the squeeze finger action at delivery. Then you cannot top the ball!*

Cure for the fault of a backswing with an outside arc: Pay careful attention to keeping your arm close to your side all through the delivery, both during the backswing and during the forward swing. Do not let the right shoulder drop unnecessarily low because, if you do, the weight of the ball may cause it to get away from you.

Here I am demonstrating the fault of dropping the right shoulder. Sometimes this is caused by using a bowling ball that is too heavy for the bowler. It is natural for your right shoulder to be slightly lower because of the weight and action of the ball suspended from it by the arm. The error comes when the ball is allowed to get excessively low, which destroys your ability to remain square to the line.

BALL "GETS AWAY" FROM BODY AT DELIVERY

A major fault seen in many bowlers, even the professionals at times, is that of letting the hand and ball get out away from the body at the delivery point. This fault usually happens when the bowler fails to maintain his straight approach to the line. He *slants* in toward the center of the lane, and realizing that he has slanted in, he makes either

I am working with Cathy on her fault of slanting. Notice that her right foot has moved in several boards to the left on her first step toward the line. Her squareness to the line has immediately been destroyed. The only way she can recover is to slant back out to the right, and the result will be an erratic delivery without accuracy or power.

one or the other of two mistakes. If he maintains his approach to the left, he releases the ball to the left and not on his intended line. Second, he may realize that he has slanted in and still wants to roll the ball down his intended line. The only way he can do that is to let his arm wander out from his body away from his sliding foot at the delivery point. From that angle little or no action can be imparted to the ball.

Here is a subsequent picture of Cathy as she works on her problem of slanting. Notice that she has now been able to walk a straighter line toward the foul line. The use of a white line in the recreation room will help any bowler straighten out his footwork. The bowler who wishes to succeed must have good consistent footwork.

Cure for the fault of letting the ball "get away" from your sliding foot: Make sure your approach is straight and that your arm stays close to your body during the backswing and downswing. Stay square to the line at all times.

RUSHING THE LINE

Another frequent fault is that of rushing the line. The telltale sign here is that the sight of the bowler's foot turning clockwise at the explosion point and his body turning to the right of the pins. This is

Here I am showing the fault of a backswing that is too high. This usually happens when the bowler has too high a pushaway at the start and the momentum of the ball carries it too far into the backswing. When the backswing is too long, the bowler has difficulty retaining control of it and often has too much speed to carry the pins properly. The solution is to shorten the pushaway to normal distance and allow the backswing to go no higher than shoulder height.

usually caused by footwork that is too fast. The body gets ahead of the ball and the arm never has a chance to catch up and be in a position to make a sound release at the line. Sometimes this happens when the

Here I am demonstrating the fault of holding the ball too low. This will cause either a lifting of the ball during the pushaway or will result in holding the ball back and having little pushaway at all. In turn, the result will be an early, short, or low backswing that will not develop any power. There will be bad timing and balance, too. The ball should be slightly to the right of body center at about waist height for the best results.

bowler delays the start of his backswing a fraction of a second. The feet get moving and are out of synchronization with the arc of the ball.

Cure for the fault of rushing the line: Take your first step slowly and gradually increase your tempo on your way to the line. Have the feeling that you are behind the ball and controlling it, not the other way around with the ball forcing you to deliver it because of its weight and momentum. Take your time! It is always easier to speed up a delivery than it is to slow it down.

13
WHAT TO DO WHEN YOU ARE IN TROUBLE: A CHECKLIST

Every bowler gets into trouble at some time during a bowling session. I have had it happen to me many times in my long career and I have learned how to cope with the problem most of the time.

Recently on national television I was bowling in the final round of the greater Hartford Open championship in Windsor Locks, Connecticut. Since I had finished first in the qualifying rounds, I would bowl only in the last two games and either be the winner or runner-up. My opponent was Tommy Milton, an excellent bowler and a dangerous opponent.

I rolled the first ball and to my dismay found that although I had put the ball in the pocket with the speed and angle I wanted, the horrible 8–10 split remained standing.

My first thought was, "What did I do wrong?" At once I began my checklist of probable causes of the split. Did I slow my ball up a trifle? Did I miss my spot at the darts, let the ball get inside and therefore hit the pins more on the nose? Did I release the ball with my customary finger action? Did I cut short my follow-through? All of these thoughts ran through my mind as fast as you can say them. I also considered the fact that the leave might have been a freak one in which the pins acted peculiarly—moving straight out, wrapping around the 10-pin and 8-pin instead of tumbling and going sideways to increase the width of the swath.

I came to the conclusion that I might have rolled my first ball a little too cautiously, slower than usual, but that my line and angle were the proper ones for the particular lane conditions.

Fortunately, my analysis was correct. I came back with consecutive strikes and had solved my problem. Unfortunately for me Tom Milton continued to bowl extremely well; he doubled in the tenth frame to squeeze me out of my forty-second championship title by one mark. That first frame freak hit—or else my own failure to roll with my customary speed—cost me the championship. I'll never know which one was truly the cause.

Everyone runs into trouble occasionally in bowling, even the best bowlers. All of a sudden the ball that worked so well last week is jumping into the headpin, leaving nothing but splits; or else it is failing to come up when you expect that it will and you find yourself missing usually easy spares.

What to do? The first thing is, don't get panicky and start to make radical changes. The first consideration is whether the difficulty lies in lane conditions or in your own ability to roll your usual type of delivery. Presume first that lane conditions are at fault and make your first correction by changing your angle as indicated in our earlier discussion. At the same time, without changing your delivery other than the slight change in starting position, line, or spot, make sure that you are throwing a live ball, one with action as a result of the proper application of the squeeze.

You may make a complete correction immediately and start scoring well at once. On the other hand, you may be in serious trouble and be faced with problems with both lane conditions and your own form, so that the corrections may not work right away or at all. You must realize that sometimes it will be impossible for you to make the necessary corrections, and if that is so, reconcile yourself to a bad night and make the best of it. If you just can't get strikes, get every possible spare you can. If you are splitting frequently, try missing the headpin on the right (you'll find it hard to do) and then count your spare.

When every correction you can think of fails to work, make a radical change. If you have been bowling fairly close to the center of the lane, move way over to the corner. Do something, if only to help you to relax your tension.

Here is a checklist of things to do when you get in trouble. Photocopy this suggestion list and put in your wallet. You should read it carefully and adopt the same procedure. If you use it, it may save you many a bad night. Always try to have one of those "good" bad nights, one of those series when you escape with a respectable score when you know you shouldn't have!

A Checklist for What to Do When You Are in Trouble

1. Is my wrist firm, with the thumb on the inside pointing toward my usual thumb clock position, 10 or 11 o'clock? Is my grip secure, firm but relaxed?

2. I will check my starting position and my finishing position. Am I drifting right or left? Have I moved my starting position or my target at the line without realizing it?

3. Am I rushing the line? Are my hips square to the line at delivery? Am I sliding straight at the line?

4. Have I speeded the ball up or slowed it down without realizing it?

5. Am I releasing my thumb properly and is the ball going out over the line with the squeeze applied? Are my fingers clenched after the ball is delivered, or is my hand open?

6. Am I actually seeing the ball go over its target on the lane, or am I pulling out of the ball, cutting short my follow-through?

7. Am I pointing the ball into the headpin, trying to aim the ball rather than let it roll?

8. Is my elbow wandering from my body, causing a *side-arm* or *topping* of the ball?

9. Am I dropping the ball before I get it out over the foul line? Or am I lofting the ball too far out over the foul line?

10. Am I taking into consideration the fact that the lanes may be running more than they were at the start? Should I change my line or target?

11. I resolve to be more deliberate and take my time about each successive delivery.

14
SPECIAL TIPS FOR THE HIGH AVERAGE BOWLER

I believe that any male bowler who is presently averaging around 165 pins or a female bowler with an average of at least 150 pins should be considered a "better bowler"—one who has already learned the basics of bowling, who has developed an individual style that he or she can repeat frame after frame.

If you are presently scoring in even higher ranges than these, then I believe your chances for success are even greater. I promise you better bowlers that if you are able to adopt one or more of my special tips for the high average bowler you will inevitably improve your average from 10 to 20 pins in a season. First of all, let me say that these "Anthony super-secrets" I am about to suggest to you took me hundreds, perhaps thousands of hours of practice to perfect. So if you are not willing to devote a great deal of time and effort to these variations, I recommend that you settle for the basic bowling form you now have.

The first super-secret is that sometimes you should let your left foot *not* slide straight at the foul line. Almost by accident, many years ago I discovered while practicing my bowling that I had rolled a particularly strong strike ball. I had been observing the action of my sliding foot at the time. I would hold my delivery at the line until the ball hit the pins, then I would look down to check my sliding foot. To my amazement, I noticed that on that unusually explosive strike ball I had turned my foot in a clockwise fashion at the line. For the right-handed bowler that would mean a counterclockwise turn say from 12 o'clock to about 10 o'clock on a clock dial.

I reasoned that by making such a turn of my sliding foot just as I reached the end of my slide, I was moving the weight of my body even more than normal to the inside and allowing my hand to get under the ball a little bit more—which let it impart even more lift at the explosion point. Another interesting thing I noted was that when I performed the turned-foot measure it almost ensured that my ball would not get away from my body but would pass as close to my sliding foot as it could. It took me a great deal of practice to perfect the move. There are so many things to think about as you make a bowling delivery that it is hard to make your body obey your mind at that last split second of your slide. The move must be made about one foot from the final stopping point of your sliding foot. Try it yourself. If you can perfect it and use it when you really need that extra stuff on the ball it should help you as it did me.

The second super secret I will expose to you is the trick of *killing your ball* when you want to do so. Often it happens that lanes run so much as a result of dirt on their surfaces or a breakdown of the surfacing materials that the bowler finds no matter what he does he simply cannot keep his ball off the nose.

I picked this trick up from a low average bowler who was murdering the pins one night when I couldn't hit the headpin to save my life. I noticed that this fellow with a "nothing" ball was getting the strikes. I watched him and realized that his delivery was flawed, that his arm swing was not at a true right angle to his body and the line to the pins. He was pushing his ball out toward the center of the lane and then bringing his arm outside his body on the backswing. His plane, though faulty, was repeatedly the same.

In my next practice session I resolved to try to do the same thing he was doing. I tried putting the ball a few degrees inside my normal line and letting my arm swing go slightly outside. I tried it again and again and once more I was amazed to find that I had discovered a new way—for me, that is—to kill the ball.

The loss of lift was happening because my hand was on the side of the ball in a slightly broken-wrist position. Also, my hand at the explosion point was not as close to my sliding foot as it normally would be. Basically, I had found the reverse of the first secret, the turned-in foot. I call this shot "the 11 o'clock shot" because I visualize a clock dial with the hands pointing to 5 o'clock and 11 o'clock and my arm in its backswing on a line with 5 o'clock. (Remember I'm talking to you as a right-handed bowler; actually my dial is set at 1 o'clock and 7 o'clock.)

This shot will effectively kill the ball: give you a ball with little action at the very end of the shot. It is a useful way to get the 10-pin on a running lane. It is also invaluable on extremely running lanes where I must delay my hit.

A third super secret I call my "1 o'clock shot." In this variation I put my ball and arm swing on a 1 o'clock–7 o'clock axis in its backswing rather than on its normal square-to-the-line axis of 12 o'clock–6 o'clock. When I let my arm swing come inside I find that my arm remains even closer to my body and the ball, too, is very close alongside my sliding foot. I get considerably more leverage when it comes from that position. In this 1 o'clock shot I do not let my body turn away from square to the line, just my arm swing. It is a difficult maneuver to accomplish, even for me. If you find yourself unable to perfect this move or any of my earlier suggestions, do not be surprised or upset. It took me years to perfect them and even now I cannot count on the results I want every time.

This is the clock dial that the bowler should see in his imagination as he makes the counterclockwise turn of his sliding foot at the line in order to put more power into his shot. Practice this move without looking down at your foot. In your mind's eye see it moving from straight ahead to the 11 o'clock position.

15
BOWLING IN SAFETY

BLISTERS: PREVENTION AND REPAIR

It is obvious that your bowling ball must leave your fingers as you deliver it out over the line. The result is that somewhere on one or more of your fingers you will develop a callus or wear spot from the constant friction of the ball and your fingers. If you are using a properly-fitted bowling ball your chances of developing a blister are remote. But it often happens that the beginner bowler must suffer through a badly-fitted ball for a while and will sometimes raise a blister on one of his fingers.

Besides, many people have tender skin which blisters more quickly than normal skin does. In order to prevent any finger damage, most

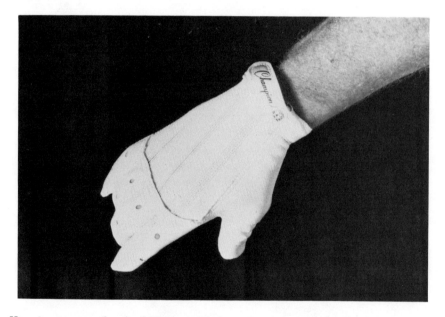

Here is an example of a full-fingered glove that a bowler might wish to wear to protect his fingers from abnormal wear on the skin. It is absolutely necessary that the glove be skintight and truly "fit like a glove." If there is any slack in the thumb, particularly, your thumb release may be hung up in the ball—and you don't want that to happen. Find the right glove for you and then stick with it!

bowlers buy and keep with them, at all times, a simple repair kit for their fingers. There are several preparations on the market based on collodion, a clear liquid which hardens and seals upon application to the skin. The potential blister spot is first underlaid with a tiny patch of cotton batting or a fine mesh cloth and then a first coat of collodion is applied. That is allowed to harden for a minute or so and then another clear coat is applied on top of the first.

There is a true art to such finger repair! The coating cannot be too thick or it will change the size of the finger-hole, nor can it be too thin or it will not last very long in action.

I recommend that you buy a finger repair kit and keep it in your bowling bag for use at any crucial time. Be sure to use it *before* a blister

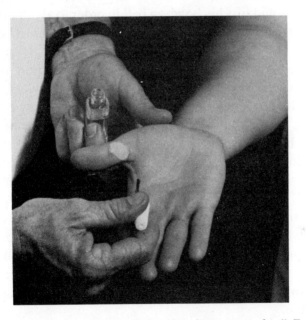

This is an illustration of the use of the "bowler's repair kit." Every bowler should have one and use it before trouble comes. The basis is collodion, a viscous liquid that hardens and leaves a protective coating on the finger. The little pads provide a foundation to strengthen the repair and make it last longer in use.

occurs, because once you have a blister you will have a long painful recovery period and probably will not be able to bowl your usual game until the blister is healed.

Ask your lane manager or bowling professional to show you how to make a finger repair. I'm sure he's had lots of experience and can give you practical advice on how to do it.

THAT HEAVY BALL: HOW TO TRANSPORT/MOVE/LIFT

As you know, your bowling ball weighs 16 pounds. In many different ways those 16 pounds can become a dangerous instrument capable of causing anything from painful injury to complete incapacitation of a bowler. Every bowler must be extremely careful of the way he transports, moves, and lifts his bowling ball in order to avoid the possibility of back injury, muscle strain, or a crushing accident to his fingers or toes.

Going from your house to the bowling lane, transport your bowling ball in one of the bags specially constructed for bowlers. These bags are an absolute necessity for every bowler because they carry not only the ball but also all kinds of extra gear that the bowler needs to bowl well and to bowl safely: your shoes; your extra pair of short socks; your bowling glove or gloves; your repair kit, the bottle of collodion and patches for the repair of a blistered finger; a hand towel; and "your little black book," your bible which helps you to figure out the performance tricks and tracks of the various lanes.

The bowling bag and its contents usually weigh from 20 to 22 pounds. It is a heavy object in itself; and when it is in the trunk of an automobile down inside the rear ledge of the trunk, it offers a formidable problem to the bowler to lift it out safely without straining an arm or back muscle.

My advice to you is to never attempt to lift your heavy bowling bag while your body is stretched out at great length. Always try to lift it in the easiest way possible. If the ball lies away from the edge of the trunk, ease it slowly toward you, and then instead of reaching in with one hand and lifting the bag up with one hand only, brace your body firmly on both feet, reach in with both hands, and lift the bag straight up in the fashion of a weight lifter making a forward press of a set of barbells. Both hands and arms should exert equal upward pressure. If you lift your ball out of your car this way you most likely will not injure yourself.

Another tip for you on carrying your bowling bag in the trunk of your car: Without some bracing it is apt to become a 20-pound loose missile in your trunk as your car makes a sudden turn or stops at high speed. It can pick up some of the momentum of the car and crash around in your trunk. The answer I have found is to get a wooden box slightly larger than the ball bag. When the bag is seated in a box it will not escape and cause trouble. Put a towel under the ball, too, for even more safety.

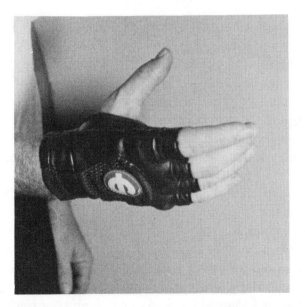

This is a wrist protector of the type that I myself wear to help take the strain of the weight of the ball in the backswing. It acts as a wrist strengthener and will also prevent wrist strain. I recommend that you try this type yourself. It will help you bowl with more physical ease and prevent any unwanted injury.

MOISTURE: PROBLEMS AND SOLUTIONS

When your bowling ball remains in the trunk of your car and the outside temperature goes down, you will find that moisture will condense on the ball as soon as you take it out of the bag in the bowling lane. That's an unpleasant situation—a cold wet bowling ball, not to mention the ice-cold bowling shoes you have to put on. There are several answers to the problem. One, put some antimoisture tablets in your bag so that the tablets will pick up the water instead of your ball. Two, try not to leave your ball in your car long enough to get cold. This may mean extra handling of the bag in and out of your car, but trust me, it's worth it.

Damp Shoes

Now, about moisture: It is a bowler's dreaded enemy. If your shoes are damp they will stick on the lane. If your sliding foot sticks you can cause any one of several injuries. First, you may stop dead in your tracks while your body may remain in motion because of the momentum of your approach. That will cause your sliding foot, and especially your left big toe, to turn back on itself unnaturally. You may tear a tendon in your foot. If you do, you won't bowl for three to six weeks and the memory of that pain will remain for years, every time you stick again at the lane (as all bowlers do once in a while).

Be very careful then about getting water on the soles of your shoes, especially on the sole of your sliding foot. There are many places where spilled water or a spilled soft drink can leave moisture ready to entrap you. On a rainy or snowy night at the bowling lanes be extra watchful. Look out for one of your fellow bowlers to track in water on his street shoes. Many bowlers are careless about this hazard, so you must take that into consideration. As you begin your routine preparatory to rolling either your first or second ball, make it your regular practice to put your sliding foot on the lane and in a mock slide, testing it to make sure the shoe will slide properly. Then you can proceed with the rest of your routine with an unhurried mind. This is also an excellent reminder to yourself to slide properly at the line. Your knee should be bent, the sole only touching the pin deck; your heel up in the air, not touching the lane. You are saying to yourself, "This is a rehearsal of the way I want to slide at the line."

SAFE FINGERS

I want to warn you also about the danger of crushing your fingers between bowling balls or between your bowling ball and scorer's table. Many years ago when the ball returns came straight back from the lane, I went to the ball rack to pick up my ball. I did it in the approved, safe way with my hands on either side of the ball. Just as I had retrieved my ball and had taken it no more than a foot away from the rack and was holding it about waist high, another ball came crashing into the other balls on the return rack. The sight and sound of the crash caused me to think for a second, "My finger is in between there!" and, startled, I dropped my ball on my left big toe. I cannot describe the resulting pain. I actually was able to finish the game — it was my last of three — and then the throbbing started in earnest. I did not break the toe, but bruised it badly. I never did that again, you can be sure, but I will never forget that day and how it happened.

So be careful not to get your fingers between the balls on the return rack or carousel. Always lift your ball out from the side of the ball return rack using your nonbowling hand and arm. That lessens the work your bowling hand and arm have to do during the bowling session.

AN OUNCE OF PREVENTION

Be careful when you bowl. Don't run the risk of injuring yourself. There is no reason for you ever to hurt your back, your toes, or your fingers if you follow these sensible instructions on safety. Don't let the conduct of another bowler cause any injury to yourself.

When I go to a drinking fountain or into a bar at a bowling lane while I am bowling, I have found it useful to adopt a peculiar gait with my sliding leg (my right, of course, but for you it would be your left). I keep the sliding sole of my right foot up in the air and allow only the heel to touch the floor. In this way I make sure the sliding foot does not pick up any water. The same walking trick can and should be used on a trip to the toilet during a game. It is even more important then to see that you do not step into water.

Good bowlers constantly check the soles of their shoes not only for water but for the presence of any other foreign material such as gum or candy. Make it your regular habit to check your sliding foot every time you leave the immediate vicinity of your bowling lane, banquettes, or seats near the scorer's table.

16
ETIQUETTE OF BOWLING

To paraphrase an adage of golf, "Bowling is a gentleman's game played by ladies and gentlemen." Bowling has a very old, well-defined code of etiquette which is observed by every knowledgeable bowler who has good manners.

The first rule is that no one ever intentionally distracts another bowler while he is in the act of bowling—either by infringing in his territory on the lane, by talking to him or shouting at him, by making distracting noises, or in general, by any conduct which would tend to keep the other bowler from concentrating on rolling the ball down the lane.

For that reason, it is generally agreed that the bowler on the right-hand lane of a pair of lanes has the right-of-way. In most cases he should proceed to bowl before the bowler on the left-hand side of the pair. This right-of-way can always be waived by the right-hand bowler. He merely indicates by a gesture that he would rather wait and let the bowler on his left go first.

You should be aware, too, of the bowler's superstition against "rolling into a split." For years there has been an unwritten law of etiquette in bowling that if you happen to draw a split you will clear it as fast as you can to get it out of the sight of the other bowlers.

So even if the bowler in the right-hand lane has the right-of-way to bowl first, if you happen to have left a wide-open split on the left-hand lane, don't be surprised if the bowler on the right-hand side sits down or otherwise indicates he will not bowl until you have cleared your split. Incidentally, another interesting bowling superstition is that an open split in your first frame means you will roll a 200 game. I don't believe it myself but perhaps the basis for it is psychological: if you think you shouldn't be discouraged by the split, you will not be.

Traffic on the bowling lanes can often be compared to a driver trying to find a safe opening to cross a fast-moving highway. The bowler has to look right and left, gauge the state of those bowlers at the line, consider whether any bowler will jump around and distract him, decide that he won't—and then proceed to make his own methodical approach.

Do not ever pick up your bowling ball from the return rack while another bowler is preparing to bowl and is in his starting position. You may be out of his direct line of sight but the movement of the balls on the track may make enough commotion to distract him and upset him.

If the antics of some bowler bothers you, I would advise you to consistently give way to him and let him bowl first even if under normal etiquette you could bowl first.

A good point of bowling etiquette is shown here. The bowler on my left should not step on the lane approach until I have made my delivery. As a general rule, the bowler on the right-hand side of a pair of lanes always has the right of way.

If you are bowling on a team and cannot bowl some night, it is of paramount importance that you tell your captain well in advance so that he can arrange for a substitute in your place. Many leagues have lists of regular substitutes; it is even more polite if you can tell your captain you have already arranged for a sub to take your place.

Failure to appear for bowling without prior notice is extremely impolite. Your team is usually penalized by having a "Mr. Average's" score entered as the missing bowler's score, and a 10-pin penalty is often assessed.

It is not only polite but part of the fun of bowling to participate enthusiastically in the fortunes of your team. Cheer the good bowlers or lucky ones as the case may be. Do not deride the bad ones, but commiserate with them. Don't ever needle another bowler about his misses or splits. It is very bad form and will cause you to lose a lot of friends, some of them your own team members.

Scorekeeping is a burdensome task for anyone. Volunteer your services when you feel it is your turn to keep score, and be alert at all times to help the scorekeeper. He has to bowl himself so when he leaves the scoresheet, take over for him until he returns. Help him as he goes along by reporting the number of pins knocked down on various first balls.

It is always good sportsmanship to remind a bowler—friend or foe—that he has a hidden pin, "a mother-in-law," on a spare. And if you have the good luck to be present when a bowler strings strikes together and nears a perfect 300 game, don't say a word about it to anyone for fear you'll break his lucky streak. It is another part of the etiquette of bowling to be quiet about an impending 300. I hope some day there is a great silence over your 300—and then a houseful of cheers!

17
THE LANGUAGE
OF BOWLING

No longer do we have bowling alleys, they are *lanes*. The trough on the sides of a lane is no longer the gutter, it is now the *channel*. Bowlers are not bowlers anymore, they are now *players* on nationally televised bowling matches. However, in spite of the efforts to up-grade bowling terminology, a bowler who rolls his ball from the extreme right or left edge of the lane is still said to be making a *gutter shot*.

The language of bowling is most colorful. The game has a pleasant jargon all its own, and if you learn it and understand it you will find that your pleasure in the game will be greatly enhanced. You can join the crowd in criticism and applause of the bowlers around you, and knowing the language, you will be so much more a part of this great game.

A great many bowling terms describe various types of bowling ball action. A good way to teach you some of the language of bowling is to show you how it's used in actual play. So here goes:

As you enter the bowling lane and put your bowling bag down, if one of your teammates laughingly tells you, "Don't get that water all over me!" he's merely referring to your bad night last week when you threw a *water ball*, a *pumpkin*, a *flat one*, or a *tomato*.

You start to bowl and the first ball you throw is a slow curve. Though it just barely touches the headpin, all the pins start to dance and tumble down for a strike. Someone calls out, "You pulled the rug out from under that one!" or "You really stole that one," or "You're not going to take that strike, are you?" And soon after, you roll a strike on a ball that normally you expect to hook into the headpin—but instead of hooking, it holds a direct line and at the last moment seems to *set,* driving high and hard on the headpin for a strike. You come back to the seats and say, "Boy, was that a tight one! I was a little scared until it *set!*" Or if all the pins flew solidly backward into the pit you might say, "Was that a *crasher!*"

A *solid* hit is one right in the 1–3 pocket with such force and authority that usually a strike results. So it follows that a *solid 10-pin* is one that is left standing after a *solid* smash. Don't be ashamed of *taps,* that is, leaving a 10-pin or a 4-pin or a 7-pin on what appears to be a good hit. A pin off-spot a fraction of an inch one way or the other, or erratic ball action at the last moment, can cause strange pin action and the loss of a strike that you might normally expect to get. Take your time and concentrate on converting the single-pin spare, for all too many lone pins are missed merely because the bowler—still rankling over the injustice of having left the single pin stranded on a good hit—forgets to concentrate and *blows the spare*.

When you get your second strike in a row, you have *doubled;* you are now *working on a big one*. And when you get your third strike in a row you have a *turkey* or *triple*. More strikes in a row give you a *string* of strikes—one of the pleasures of bowling, especially when you get a lucky *Brooklyn* or *Jersey* hit in the opposite pocket, the 1–2 instead of the 1–3. There'll be more groans from your team as they say, "Don't be embarrassed, take it and sit down!"

And then come the splits: the *baby splits* are the 3-10, which a right-handed bowler draws frequently on a *high* hit, one that goes into the headpin too much toward the center; and the 2-7, usually drawn by the left-hander on a similar hit for him. The nasty 4-6-7-10, the two pins on each far side of the lane, is called variously *double pinochle* or *the big four*. The 8-10 is called a *strike split* because it results from what seems to be a good 1-3 pocket hit. No matter what it is called it is one of the *impossibles*.

Lanes are *running* when you can't hold your ball off the headpin; *stiff* when you can't make your ball curve and *come up* to the headpin. They are *soft* lanes when you score well on them; *rough* or *tough* or *mean* when they are hard to score on.

When you have a spare leave such as the 2–8 or the 3–9 your fellow bowlers will tell you that your *mother-in-law* is in the back row or may say, "Watch out, you've got a *sleeper*." The 1–2–4–7 leave is a *picket fence* and so is its counterpart, the 1–3–6–10. The appearance of that spare will tell you how it got its name. Interestingly, a 5–7 split is a *Kresge* but its counterpart, the 5–10, is a *Woolworth*.

Always remember that the pins are called in their numerical sequence from the low number to the high number. That means that if you leave a spare such as the headpin, the next pin to it on the right, and the 10-pin, you would call it the 1–2–10 and not the 10–2–1 or the

2-1-10. It follows, too, that the *double pinochle* split is always called the 4-6-7-10, reading the numbers in the front row from left to right and then those in the back row. Not long ago I happened to hear one of the announcers on a television show call the numbers of a split in the wrong sequence. Every knowledgeable bowler in the country who heard him knew at once that this announcer didn't know the sport very well and probably was faking his expertise.

Perhaps you will originate a new bowling term some day yourself!

BOWLING LITERATURE

When I first started to bowl I went to my local library to see what books had been written on bowling instruction. The sports selection was not a large one. There were just two books on bowling: one by Joe Wilman, a bowling champion of those early days and one by Ned Day, probably the first celebrity bowling champion of the modern day. I took both books out and read them voraciously. Later on I was able to buy a copy of Day's book. I still have it and still read it once in a while.

It is amazing how little those books told about the art of bowling. They were very rudimentary in their advice, but they did serve to create interest in better bowling.

In the last 20 years many, many excellent books on bowling instruction have been written. I recommend that you read as many of them as you can. In particular: If you are interested in the fine points of the game and especially the problems of ball balance and ball fit, you should read Bill Taylor's book, *Fitting and Drilling a Bowling Ball*—a true masterpiece of research. Another wonderful addition to the literature of bowling is *The Complete Guide to Bowling Spares* by Dick Ritger and George Allen. There you will find hundreds more spares than I have discussed here in this book. Another excellent book aimed at the high average bowler is *Weber on Bowling* by Dick Weber, a great modern-age bowling champion who has a lot of sensible ideas on how to play the lanes.

18
BOWLING FOR
LEFT-HANDERS

A left-handed bowler usually tries to learn the proper techniques of the game by doing exactly the opposite of the instructions for right-handed bowlers. In many situations this works very well but there's more of a difference between right-handers and left-handers in bowling than just rolling the ball with different hands.

Because of lane conditions and the greater number of bowlers who bowl right-handed, there is often an advantage to bowling left-handed provided that the left-hander understands his own game.

As I have pointed out in my instructions for right-handers, the usual starting point for a right-handed bowler is to line himself up and attempt to roll his first ball over the second arrow from the right. The left-hander, you will find, is able to stand much farther to the left on the approach than the right-hander can on his right. There is a *track*—or constantly used portion—on the right-hander's side of the lane while the left-hander, because of considerably less play on his side of the lane, has what I call a *virgin track*.

There are benefits and detriments to having the virgin track. The first detriment is that sometimes the track for the right-hander amounts to a slot which will almost automatically bring the right-hander's ball into the pocket. The left-hander does not get such a slot or help from the lane bed. He has to follow his own line without benefit of help from the lane.

The benefit to the left-hander is that he has a much better angle into the strike pocket—the 1–2 for him—by rolling his ball over the first arrow from the left. This angle results in less deflection of the ball as it hits the pocket. Remember that the 5-pin is truly the target pin and the more directly the ball can get to it, the better the bowler's chance for a strike. The left-hander's ball, coming in from farther outside on the lane, heads more directly for the 5-pin. If it is deflected as a result of low velocity or lack of finger action the ball may still get to the 5-pin and take it out.

While the left-hander will bowl from a greater outside angle than the right-hander will, I recommend that every left-hander learn to play all the angles just as the right-hander must learn them. Remaining in the left corner or far left may not always be the best angle for a left-hander. When the left-hander learns all the angles he is prepared for any lane conditions he may encounter. He becomes the complete bowler without any weaknesses.

The left-hander, oddly enough, seems to have more of a tendency to pull the ball or point it toward the 1–2 pocket. The problem may be mental, and may be related to an unconscious realization by the bowler as he reaches the foul line that he is fairly well out toward the left—perhaps too far—and the result is that he instinctively compensates for the fear and pulls the ball across his body.

The left-hander must be more careful than the right-hander to keep his bowling elbow in close to his hip so that his arm swing will be straight through without any sign of pull to the right.

From my experience, I have observed that the middle average left-handers become more proficient sooner than right-handers because they have fewer factors to contend with, such as the lane track, angle, and deflection. Since the left-hander is able to roll the ball the same way most of the time, he is able to learn his own game more quickly.

Let me give you left-handers this sound advice: You do not have to make major adjustments the way right-handers do. Normally you need not play a lane any deeper or more inside than the second arrow. When the lanes are exceptionally dry—that is, without any oil or without much oil—the left-hander will necessarily have to move farther inside and roll the ball farther out to the left in order to hit the strike pocket. Regardless of the conditions, roll the ball through the target area. With proper adjustment of speed you should still be an effective strike shooter.

I believe that I have an advantage in bowling left-handed, that my ball has a consistently truer reaction on the pins because of the absence of a lane track on my side. Sometimes, though, when I see a right-hander carrying lots of strikes on a *slot alley,* as it is called, I get extremely jealous and wish for a while that I were not cursed with my natural left-handedness.

Here are some photos showing me bowling my natural left-handed delivery. In this first one, taken in the midst of my backswing, I want you to observe my intense concentration on my target out on the lane.

In this photo I am standing toward the explosion point of the delivery at the line. Notice how I have leaned forward and that my sliding leg is bent, my shoulders definitely square to the line as I concentrate on my target.

In this photo the ball has just come off my fingers after they have executed the squeeze. My hand and arm are coming straight up, my body is still square to the line, and my knee is still bent as the slide is completed. I am still intent upon my target and will watch to see the ball hit my spot at the break of the boards.

Here is a photo of my full finish with my hand and arm high. My fingers are still clenched after executing the squeeze at delivery. I would like you to pay particular attention to my balance at the line. You, too, should be able to reach this perfectly balanced position and be able to look down at your sliding foot to check that your slide was straight toward your target line.

We cannot change the way we were born. If you are left-handed, there is no reason why you cannot bowl as well or better than your fellow bowlers. Accept your fate and make the most of it.

19
BOWLING FOR WOMEN

The Woman's International Bowling Congress reports that there are more than 168,000 leagues of women bowlers in the United States at this time. Although it is difficult to get an exact count it is believed that there are another 24 million women who do not bowl in organized

I am cautioning Cathy about dropping her shoulder and letting the ball get away from her side. Most women, in my opinion, try to roll a ball that is too heavy for them to handle. I suggest that the woman bowler start with a fairly light ball and then work up to the heaviest one she can handle with comfort and without strain.

leagues but do bowl occasionally with their families in so-called open bowling.

All the foregoing instructions on the art and science of bowling are equally applicable to the woman bowler, with a single important exception: While I recommend that the male bowler use a 16-pound

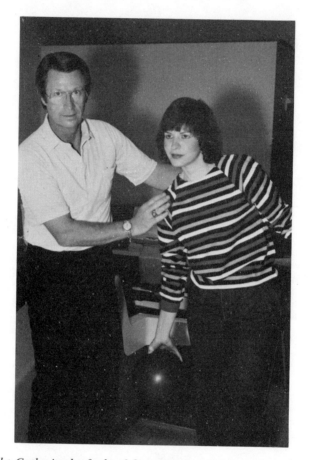

I have caught Cathy in the fault of dropping her shoulder. Notice how the ball gets away from the body when this happens. Many women use bowling balls that are so heavy for them that they are forced to drop their shoulders. A well-fitted bowling ball of proper weight is most important for success by the woman bowler.

ball, the heaviest possible under the rules, I do not recommend that the woman bowler use as heavy a ball.

Most women are not as strong as their counterparts in male bowling and so they must compensate for their lack of great physical strength by learning to bowl with accuracy. Women bowlers should use bowling balls in the 12- to 14-pound range at first, then as control is achieved, more weight in ounce increments can be added judiciously to the ball until the ideal maximum of weight and control is reached.

Remember that a lighter ball will deflect more when it strikes the pins. This is an advantage for the woman bowler attacking a 1–3–6–10 clothesline spare. Her ball will bounce off the headpin and right down the line to clear up the spare handily. But the lighter ball simply will not get into the heart of the pin setup and rout out that

Here I am showing Cathy how important it is that she not allow her wrist to break downward as she starts her delivery. Many women do not have strong wrists. That is why I recommend the use of a wrist protector for women for their comfort and to give them good results in their bowling deliveries.

important 5-pin. As a result of greater deflection and less carrying power in the lighter ball the woman bowler must necessarily bowl more from the corner, more directly at the 1–3 pocket and at the 5-pin beyond the 1–3.

I have found that women often have naturally weaker wrists than

Here I am instructing Cathy on the proper way to hold her elbows close to her side in order to give her compactness in her delivery. The ball should be held slightly to the right side to enable it to drop away easily in a pendulum swing that is straight back and then straight forward.

men do. So, to combat that problem I suggest that the woman bowler wear a wrist protector, such as the one I use, to help keep her wrist from breaking down in the backswing under the weight of the ball.

I have observed that many women bowlers roll in too ladylike a fashion to exert any authority on the bowling ball and on the pins.

Here I am instructing Cathy on the importance of bending the left knee as she slides to the line. Without a proper knee-bend it is impossible for the body to reach forward and put the ball out on the lane. The slide must be straight, too, in order to allow the bowler to roll down the preselected target line.

Therefore, the woman bowler should do everything she can to increase the speed of her delivery so that she can overcome the problem of the lighter ball and greater deflection at the pins. Remember that the speed of delivery is governed by the height and actual "push" of the pushaway as well as by the speed of the bowler's footwork to the foul line. Moving back an extra foot or so on the approach will often give the woman bowler the steam she needs.

Women bowlers need to observe all the fundamentals of championship bowling just as the men do. Be careful with body alignment, with rhythm and timing, and be sure to impart the squeeze at the explosion point and follow through for as many strikes as the men get!

Many women bowlers hold the ball too high at the start of their delivery and the result is a rushed approach with little control over the ball. A ball that is started too high will tend to go too high in the backswing, too, and will result in erratic deliveries, loss of action on the ball, and inconsistency in general.

20
BOWLING FOR THE FAMILY

It is said, "The family that prays together, stays together." I firmly believe that is true. I would like to add a comment of my own much like it concerning bowling—that is, "The family that plays together stays together and has more fun than any other family."

Through the clever device of handicapping according to current bowling averages, Dad can bowl against Mom and at the same time the kids can compete on equal terms with their parents. The result is that everyone has a marvelous time on the lanes.

Usually the parents in a bowling family are members of a regular league and therefore will have established averages. Although the children may not be bowling in a regular league it is simple to calculate their averages for handicap purposes. One of the family members should be designated secretary of the family league and given the task

Steve and Brenda Croce bowl every Sunday with their son, Jason, who is one of the youngest stars of the Palm Beach Junior Bowling League. Jason is averaging 132 pins per game. By using a handicap differential he is able to bowl successfully against his mother and father—and quite often defeat them!

of recording all the scores of the family in league play and in open competition, computing their current averages.

Let's say our typical family consists of Bob, the father; Lois, the mother; Jim, a 14-year-old son; and Joan, an 8-year-old daughter. Both Bob and Lois bowl in regular leagues—Bob with his golf club, Lois with her church. Their averages are 175 and 145 respectively. Jim

Jason Croce, four years old, already has bowled a 172 game with his 6-pound full-sized ball. See how Jason is concentrating on his target and the great squeeze action of his fingers as this ball heads for a certain strike!

bowls only in open play, not in a league, but by keeping a record of his bowling scores when he bowls with his friends he has established a 140 average. Little Joan bowls only with the family and her scores show that she is averaging 95 pins.

By establishing Bob's 175 average as par, or 100 percent, the handicaps for the other bowlers can be calculated in this way: Lois's

Dawson Taylor is seen here congratulating Scott Haefele, 10 years old, on his high game of 227 in the Junior League of Palm Beach. Scott has been bowling for five years, uses a 12-pound ball, and now carries a 172 average in his league.

145 is substracted from Bob's 175 to give her a 30 pin spot or handicap. Jim would get a spot of 175 minus 140, or 35 pins. Joan would have an 80-pin spot.

Now let me show you how those scores are entered as games are bowled. Since Lois is to receive 30 pins, the third, sixth, and ninth frame counts for Lois should be increased by 10 pins each. For Jim, the

Here Scott is seen in an almost perfect delivery. Notice his intense concentration on his target, his excellent body balance, his ball close to his side, and his fingers behind the ball as he nears the explosion point of his delivery. Almost perfect, Scott . . . you must stay behind that foul line!

third, sixth, and ninth frame counts could be increased by 12, 12, and 11 pins. Joan's score should have 10 extra pins added in the second through ninth frames. In this way—by spreading the marks out along the way—the excitement of a close match can be maintained. I know many families who bowl competitively against each other and have a great time. I am aware of another family of all boys, the Sullivan

Another excellent view of Scott Haefele. Notice his fine hand and wrist action and the start of his full follow-through. His fingers are closing in classic squeeze action.

family, which regularly fills its own 5-man team in one of the classic leagues. All the Sullivans have averages of 190 or more. You should see the good-natured rivalry when some of their high scores are being compiled!

When everyone in the family is a bowler a great deal more can be done in the way of practice at home, too. There is even more incentive to set up a mock lane approach in a recreation room and practice on it in order to perfect the footwork necessary for a sound bowling game.

In these days many parents wonder where their children are spending their leisure time. When you and your children are bowling together at attractive neighborhood lanes in a clean and exciting sports atmosphere it doesn't seem likely that your children will go wrong. Furthermore, if you take my suggestion about family bowling, I think you will find your family ties growing stronger and stronger. You are building a firm foundation of cameraderie that can last a lifetime.

21
DEVELOP YOUR OWN STYLE

All through this book I have told you in an emphatic way, "Put your left foot here (or there) on starting position! Bowl from this angle (or that angle)!"

Actually what this book has attempted to do is to give you various points of reference from which you can develop your own bowling style. Some people take longer steps than others. Therefore, it is entirely possible that your starting position should be from six inches to a foot or more behind the particular dot I have discussed. Or if your stride is a short one it might be best for you to start from six inches to a foot ahead of that spot.

The best way to determine the distance of your starting position from the foul line is to make your approach in reverse: With your back to the pins at the foul line, start with your left foot and walk four steps away from the pins in the stride that you would normally use in walking—no longer, no shorter. When you have reached your fourth step, stop and look down to see where your left foot is. Mark that spot on the approach with a pencil or other marking device. Now add a half-step to take into account your slide at the line, and you will have your starting position within a few inches.

Don't be afraid to alter your starting position to closer or farther away from the foul line as your game develops. Sometimes it happens that shortening your footwork a few inches will make a world of difference in the compactness of your delivery—or on the other hand, lengthening it may put additional speed on your ball and help you to carry that borderline strike. Experiment!

After you have begun to standardize your bowling delivery and can count on the same six inches or more of hook at the end of your ball track, then you can depart moderately from the exact instructions I have given you in the book. But nearly all the starting positions I have recommended for you remain valid in relation to one another and in relation to the angles which are suggested for making strikes and for converting spares and splits.

However, if you find that you can convert the 10-pin or for that matter any other pin or spare—by going completely contrary to the recommended angle, (for example, by bowling for the 10-pin from Far Right Position rather than Far Left) by all means bowl for that spare from the angle you have found successful for you. The purpose of the game is to knock down the most pins, convert the most spares and splits, and thereby get the highest total score.

There is a famous saying in golf attributed to the champion, Lloyd Mangrum: "We're not playing 'how' but 'how many'!" It fits bowling just as well as it does golf.

Along the same line of reasoning is the problem of making a straight line approach to the foul line. Some bowlers find it constitutionally impossible to walk a straight line; you may be one of them. If you find you cannot do so, it may be that the starting positions I have suggested for the straight walker are all wrong for you. You will have to build in your own correction—possibly one board to as many as six or seven boards to the right or left of the recommended starting position. But remember that if you do make such a correction, you must stay with it consistently every time. My advice to you is, "Experiment." Understand the theory and put it into practice, adapting the various suggestions to fit your own individual situation.

Some bowlers find, when bowling on the right-hand lane of a pair of lanes, that it is difficult to bowl from as far left as the Far Left Starting Position requires. The reason for this is that as the bowler delivers the ball his follow-through causes his right leg to swing around behind him and his foot—or more painfully, his unprotected ankle—strikes the ball return rack. However, this bowler finds that when he bowls on the left-hand lane of a pair of lanes he is not bothered with interference from the rack because his foot can swing freely without any rack in the way.

The problem then is whether the bowler should move farther left on the left-hand lane where there is no interference, or use the same more restricted starting position that he uses on the right-hand lane. This is an individual decision which every bowler must make for himself. Try both ways. If by using more lane on the left-hand side than the right you find you convert as many 10-pins as you should, then you have solved your problem. If not, try bowling from the left-hand spot on each lane—that may be your answer to consistent conversion of the 10-pin.

Make your decision, and once you do, stick with it. Don't try one method one day and the other another day. Build a consistent style—a methodical approach to every strike, every spare, every split based upon the sound principles I have given you.

I also recommend that you observe in action, and study carefully, the best bowlers in your bowling area. If you do, you can pick up valuable pointers on bowling style that you can add to your own bowling form. Every city has a league called a classic league with the highest average bowlers bowling *at scratch,* meaning without handicap. Find out when that league bowls in your area and attend some of the bowling sessions. Frequently such a league travels—that is, does not bowl in just one bowling league but moves from lane to lane every week. The good bowlers of such a league are ideal for your study. You can watch them deal with all kinds of lane conditions from extremely stiff to very running, from dry lane beds to heavily oiled ones. Observe the various styles. Try to find a good bowler of the same physical size and strength as yourself and watch him closely. Try to pick up his rhythm, his smoothness, his confident bowling attitude. Then, try to put the best part of his game into your own.

I want to encourage you to become a better bowler. You can do it if you want to and I sincerely hope that this book will help you to achieve an enviable ambition: to "know what you are doing" when you bowl, and then have worlds more fun doing it!

GLOSSARY

Alley: Playing surface of maple and pine boards.

All the way: Finishing a game with all strikes.

Anchorman: Last man to roll on the team.

Approach: Area behind the foul line.

Arrows: Aiming points imbedded in the lane.

Baby the ball: Deliver the ball without authority.

Baby split: The 2–7 or 3–10 split leave.

Baby split with company: The 2–7–8 or 3–9–10 split leave.

Backup: A ball that rolls or breaks to the right for right-handed bowlers, to the left for left-handed bowlers.

Balk: An incomplete approach in which the bowler does not deliver the ball but pulls up short of the foul line.

Ball track: The area of the lane where most balls roll.

Barmaid: A pin hidden behind another pin.

Bed: The alley bed, synonymous with a single lane.

Bedposts: The 7–10 split.

Beer frame: In team play, when all but one of the players scores a strike, the one who doesn't must treat. Also, any designated frame in which the bowler who scores the fewest pins must pick up a refreshment tab.

Belly the ball: Increase the width of a hook from an inside starting angle.

Bench jockeying: Any type of conversation or other action intended to upset an opponent.

Bicycle: Hidden pin, same as *barmaid*.

Big ears: The 4–6–7–10.

Big fill: Nine or ten pins on a spare or on a double strike.

Big four: The 4–6–7–10, same as *big ears*.

Blocked: A lane maintenance condition in which oil or some sort of lane finish is used to create a track.

Blow: A missed spare.

Blowout: Downing all the pins but one.

Board: A lane consists of individual strips of lumber called boards. Pros call them by number—fifth board, fifteenth board, etc.—for targeting purposes.

Break: A lucky shot. Also a stopper after a number of consecutive strikes.

Break of the boards: The area on the lane where the maple and pine boards meet. Also known as the *piano keys*.

Bridge: Distance separating finger holes.

Brooklyn: Left of headpin for a right-handed bowler. Right of headpin for a left-handed bowler.

Broom ball: A ball that hits the pocket in such a way that the pins scatter as though they were swept with a broom.

Bucket: The 2–4–5–8 spare leave for righty; 3–5–6–9 for lefty.

Channel: Depression to right and left of lane to guide ball to pit should it leave the playing surface on the way down.

Cheesecakes: Lanes on which strikes come easily.

Cherry: Knocking down the front pin of a spare leave while a pin behind and/or to the left or right remains standing.

Chop: Same as *cherry*.

Clothesline: The 1–2–4–7 or 1–3–6–10 spare leave.

Count: Number of pins knocked down on first ball of each frame.

Cranker: Bowler who uses cranking motion to roll wide hook ball.

Cross: Going to the left side for a righty. Same as *Brooklyn*. Going to the right side for a lefty.

Curve: Ball that breaks from right to left (for righty) in a huge arc (left to right for a lefty).

Dead apple, dead ball: Ineffective ball, usually fades or deflects badly when it hits the pins.

Deadwood: Pins knocked down but remaining on the lane or in the gutter. Such pins must be removed before continuing play.

Dinner bucket, dinner pail: Same as *bucket*.

Division boards: Where the pine and maple meet on a lane.

Double: Two strikes in a row.

Double pinochle: The 4–6–7–10 split, same as *big ears, big four.*

Double wood: Any two pins, when one is directly behind the other: the 1–5, 2–8 and 3–9.

Dutch 200: A 200 game scored by alternating strikes and spares.

Error: A miss, same as a *blow.*

Fast: In different sections of the country the meaning is exactly the opposite. In one area it means a lane that allows a ball to hook easily, while in another area it means a lane that holds down the hook.

Fence posts: The 7–10 split.

Field goal: Ball rolled between two pins of a wide split.

Fill: Pins knocked down following a spare.

Fit split: Any split when it's possible for the ball to hit both pins (for example, the 4–5 split).

Flat ball: Ineffective ball—few revolutions, little action.

Foul: Touching or going beyond the foul line at delivery.

Foul line: The marking that determines the beginning of the lane.

Foundation: A strike in the ninth frame.

Foundation, early: A strike in the eighth frame.

Frozen rope: A ball rolled with excessive speed almost straight into the pocket.

Full hit: A ball striking near the center of the headpin on a strike attempt or the middle of any pin you may be aiming at.

Full roller: A ball that rolls over its full circumference.

Getting the wood: Knocking down as many pins as you can on an impossible split.

Goalposts: The 7–10 split. Also called *bedposts,* or *fence posts.*

Graveyards: Low-scoring lanes. In a high-scoring center the term is applied to the lowest scoring pair of lanes.

Groove: Ball track in lane.

Gutter: Same as *channel.*

Gutter ball: A ball that goes into the gutter.

Hard way: Rolling 200 by alternating strikes and spares. Same as *Dutch 200*.

High board: Because of atmospheric conditions a board in a lane may expand or contract and change the track a bowling ball should take in that area. Most boards contract and leave a low area but the situation is called a *high board*.

High hit: Ball contacting a pin near its center.

Holding alley: A lane that resists hook action of a ball.

Hole: The 1–3 pocket, 1–2 for lefties. Also another name for *split*.

Hook: A ball that breaks to the left (RHB) or to the right (LHB).

Hook alley: A lane on which the ball will hook easily.

House ball: Bowling ball provided by center.

Inside: A starting point near the center of the lane as opposed to the outside, near the edge of the lane.

Jam: Force the ball high into the pocket.

Jersey side: To the left of the headpin.

Kickback: Vertical division boards between lanes at the pit end.

Kindling wood: Light pins.

Kingpin: The 5-pin in the heart of the pin rack.

Kitty: Money collected for misses. Used to defray expenses in tournaments or divided equally at end of season.

Kresge: While the 5–10 split is called the *Woolworth*, the 5–7 is often called the *Kresge*.

Lane: Playing surface. Same as *alley*.

Late 10: When the 10-pin hesitates, and is the last to go down on a strike.

Leadoff man: First man in a team lineup

Lift: Means giving the ball upward motion with the fingers at the point of release.

Light: Not full on the headpin, too much to the right or left.

Lily: The 5–7–10 split.

Line: The path a bowling ball takes. Also a single game of bowling.

Loafing: Not lifting or turning the ball properly with the result that the ball lags and lacks action.

Lofting: Pitching the ball well out on the lane rather than rolling it.

Looper: An extra wide hook ball, usually slow.

Loose hit: A light pocket hit which gives good pin action off the kickback.

Low: Light hit on the headpin, as opposed to a high hit.

Maples: Pins.

Mark: A strike or spare.

Match play: Tournament in which bowlers are pitted individually against each other.

Miss: An error or *blow*.

Mixer: Ball with action that causes the pins to bounce around.

Mother-in-law: The 7-pin.

Move in: Adjust start nearer center on approach.

Move out: Adjust start nearer corner position on approach.

Mule ears: The 7–10 split.

Murphy: Baby split, the 3–10 or 4–7.

Nose hit: A first ball full on the headpin.

Nothing ball: Ineffective ball.

One in the dark: The rear pin in the 1–5, 2–8 or 3–9 spare.

Open: A frame that doesn't produce a strike or spare. A miss, an error, a *blow*.

Out and in: A wide hook that is rolled from the center of the lane toward the gutter and hooks back to the pocket.

Outside: Playing lanes from near the center.

Over: In professional bowling scoring a 200 average is used as par. The number of pins above the 200 average is the number of pins over or in the black.

Over-turn: To apply too much spin to the ball and not enough finger lift.

Pack: Getting a full count of ten.

Part of the building: The remark referring to leaving the 7-, 8-, 9- or 10-pin after what seems to be a perfect hit.

Pick: To knock down only the front pin of a spare leave. Same as *cherry* or *chop*.

Pie alley: A lane that is easy to score on.

Pine: Softer wood beyond division boards, where the maple ends.

Pit: Space at the end of lane where ball and pins wind up.

Pitch: Angle at which holes in bowling ball are drilled.

Pocket: The 1–3 for righties, 1–2 for lefties.

Point: To aim more directly at the pocket, high and tight.

Poison ivy: The 3–6–10.

Pot game: Competition in which two or more bowlers post stakes and high scorer or scorers win.

Powder puff: A slow ball that fails to carry the pins.

Powerhouse: A hard, strong strike ball driving all ten pins into the pit.

Pumpkin: Bowling ball that hits without power.

Quick eight: A good pocket hit which leaves the 4–7 for righties, 6–10 for lefties.

Railroad: A wide-open split.

Reading the lanes: Analyzing the lanes to determine whether the lane hooks or holds, where the best place is to roll the ball for a high score.

Return: The track on which balls roll from pit to ball rack.

Reverse: A backup ball.

Revolutions: The turns or rotations a ball takes from the foul line to the pins.

Running lane: A lane on which the ball hooks easily.

Runway: Area behind foul line; also known as platform approach.

Sandbagger: Bowler who keeps his average low purposely in order to receive a higher handicap than he deserves.

Schleifer: Thin-hit strike where pins seem to fall one by one.

Scratch: Rolling without benefit of handicap.

Set: Ball holding in the pocket.

Short pin: A pin rolling on the alley bed which just fails to reach and hit a standing pin.

Sidearming: Allowing the arm to draw away from its proper position during back and forward swing.

Sleeper: A pin hidden behind another pin.

Slick: Highly polished lane condition which tends to hold back hook.

Slot alley: Lane on which strikes are easy.

Snake eyes: The 7–10 split.

Soft alley: A lane on which strikes are easy.

Sour apple: Weak ball, one that leaves the 5–7, 5–10 or 5–7–10 split.

Span: Distance between thumb and finger holes.

Spare: Knocking all pins down with two balls.

Spare leave: Refers to pins standing after first ball is rolled.

Spiller: A light-hit strike in which the pins seem to take a longer time than other type strikes.

Splasher: A strike where the pins go down quickly.

Splice: Where maple and pine boards join on the lane.

Split: A spare leave in which the headpin is down and the remaining combination of pins have an intermediate pin down immediately ahead of or between them.

Spot: Target on lane at which the bowler aims; a dart, a dot, a dark board, or an arrow.

Steal: Get more pins than you deserve on a strike hit.

Stiff alley: A lane that holds a hook ball back.

Strike: Get all ten pins down on the first ball.

Strike out: Finish the game with strikes.

Strike split: The 8–10 on what looks like a good strike. The 7–9 for left-handed bowlers.

String: A number of continuous strikes.

Sweeper: A wide-breaking hook which carries a strike as though the pins were pushed with a broom.

Tandem: Two pins with one directly behind the other.

Tap: When a pin stands on an apparently perfect hit.

Thin hit: A pocket hit when the ball barely touches the headpin.

Tomato: Same as *pumpkin*.

Topping the ball: When fingers are on top of the ball instead of behind or to the side at release.

Triple: Three strikes in a row.

Tripped 4: When the 2-pin takes out the 4-pin by bouncing off the kickback.

Turkey: Three strikes in a row.

Turn: Action of hand and wrist toward pocket area at point of ball release.

Under: In professional bowling scoring, a 200 average is used as par. The number of pins below the 200 average is the number of pins the bowler is under or in the red.

Venting: Drilling an extra small hole to relieve suction in the thumb hole.

Washout: The 1-2-10 or 1-2-4-10 leave. Also, 1-3-7 and 1-3-6-7 leaves.

Water in the ball: A weak ball, one that leaves an 8-10, 5-7 or 5-10.

Wood: In scoring, number of pins knocked down. (''He didn't get all the wood.'')

Woolworth: The 5-10 split.

Working ball: A ball with action which mixes the pins on an off-pocket hit and has them scrambling with each other for a strike.

X: Symbol for strike.

Yank the shot: Hanging onto the ball too long and pulling it across the body.

Zero in: Find a consistent strike line on a lane.

SUGGESTED READING LIST AND BIBLIOGRAPHY

Better Bowling, Joe Wilman, New York: Asbaones and Co., 1953

Bowlers' Guide, Dick Ritger and Judy Soutar, Milwaukee, WI: American Bowling Congress, 1976

Bowling for Boys and Girls, John J. Archibald, Chicago: Follett Publishing Co., 1963

Bowling for Women, Judy Audsley, New York: Cornerstone Library, 1964

Bowling Now, Don Russell, San Diego: A. S. Barnes and Co., 1980

Bowling the Pro Way, Don Carter, New York: Viking Press, 1975

Champions' Guide to Bowling, Dick Weber, New York: Fleet Publishing Corp., 1964

Complete Guide to Bowling Spares, Dick Ritger and George Allen, Tempe, AZ: Ritger Sports Company, 1979

Fitting and Drilling a Bowling Ball, Bill Taylor, Anaheim, CA: Taylor Publishing Co., 1975

Guide to Better Bowling, Chuck Perzano, New York: Simon and Schuster, 1974

How to Bowl Better, Ned Day, New York: Fawcett Publications, Inc., 1951

Mastering Bowling, Dawson Taylor, Chicago: Contemporary Books, Inc., 1980

Par Bowling, Thomas Kouras, Palatine, IL: Progressive Bowling Development, 1976

The Secret of Bowling Strikes, Dawson Taylor, New York: H.S. Baines & Co., 1961

Weber on Bowling, Dick Weber and Roland Alexander, Englewood Cliffs, NJ: Prentice-Hall, 1981

Winning Bowling, Earl Anthony and Dawson Taylor, Chicago: Contemporary Books, Inc., 1977